DO YOURSELF
A FAVOUR

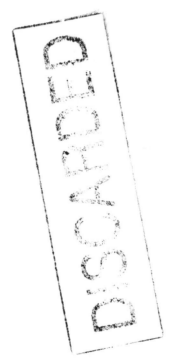

DO YOURSELF A FAVOUR

How To Be Successful At Work

Debra M. Allcock

The Industrial Society

First published in 1993 by
The Industrial Society
Robert Hyde House
48 Bryanston Square
London W1H 7LN
Telephone: 020 7479 2000

© *The Industrial Society 1993*

Reprinted 1999

ISBN 1 85835 051 4

British Library Cataloguing-in-Publication Data.
A catalogue record for this book is available from the
British Library

Typeset by: Photoprint, Torquay, Devon
Printed by: Optichrome Ltd
Cover design: Integra Communications

Cartoons: Sophie Grillet

ACKNOWLEDGEMENTS

The author would like to thank the following people for their support and assistance during the writing of this book:

Roger Salmon, Managing Director of OCS Smarts (Laundry Division); Bruce Cova MBE, Chief Executive, Sevenoaks District Council; Meg O'Brennan, Assistant to National Product Leader, the Industrial Society; and Jennifer Hammond, of Focus.

CONTENTS

INTRODUCTION

This book is about success at work.

By examining your behaviour, that of your bosses and colleagues, by looking at how you manage your time and workload, you can identify a number of common-sense, practical options to help you be more effective.

Some of the lessons in the book may seem familiar to you. You may have come across them on training courses, in other books or through your own experience of working life.

The book emphasises honesty when looking at ourselves and dealing with others. People appreciate honesty. They prefer to deal with and work with someone who is clear about themselves and their strengths and weaknesses.

The main danger you face in work is cynicism. You can encounter it from colleagues, bosses and sometimes in yourself. What you must always remember, however, is that cynics change nothing, achieve nothing, succeed at nothing. If Thomas Edison had been a cynic we would not have the electric light bulb today, if Marie Curie had been cynical she would not have discovered radium.

The percentage of effort that you put into something is usually equivalent to the percentage outcome that you get. The less you try, the less you achieve. But it isn't easy. Working life can be challenging, frustrating, irritating, sometimes boring. We all face those moments when it is easier to give up and go with the flow rather than to keep bashing away when we don't seem to be getting anywhere.

This book aims to give you a basic understanding of why things happen the way that they do and how to be more effective at work. If you understand algebra you can do algebraic sums, although you still may make mistakes. You may also make mistakes when dealing with people, but if you understand what makes them tick you will be more effective.

1 UNDERSTANDING YOURSELF

The only person who stops us doing what we want to do is ourselves. If we are clear about what we want, what motivates us, excites us, and makes us angry, we will be able to present to others a picture of ourselves which is clear, unambiguous and easier to deal with.

People are like onions. Just as onions have layers of skin, so people are made up of layers which influence behaviour and this affects how they are seen and treated by others. This is illustrated by the diagram below:

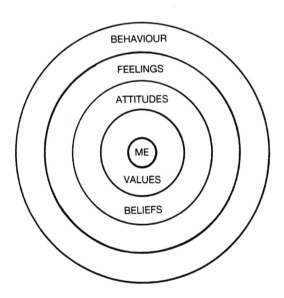

UNDERSTANDING BEHAVIOUR

VALUES

Our values are built into us throughout our lives, but primarily during our childhood years. They are influenced not just by our parents but also by our friends, teachers, people we come into contact with, books, television programmes, cinema. We have very little control over what those values are.

An example of a value we learned as a child might be that boys shouldn't cry or show emotion.

ATTITUDES AND BELIEFS

Attitudes and beliefs come directly from values. They are the way in which we judge and evaluate people and situations.

For example:	VALUE	Boys shouldn't cry or show emotion
	BELIEF/ ATTITUDE	Boys who cry are weak and immature

FEELINGS

Feelings are influenced by attitudes and beliefs. If we are in a situation where the actions of the people around us validate our values, attitudes and beliefs then we will feel good about that person or situation. If, however, we are in a situation that challenges or questions those values, attitudes and beliefs, we will feel uncomfortable and threatened.

For example:	VALUE	Boys shouldn't cry or show emotion
	BELIEF/ ATTITUDE	Boys who cry are weak and immature
	Situation:	A male colleague getting emotional and weepy
	FEELING	Uncomfortable, threatened, contemptuous.

BEHAVIOUR

Our behaviour occurs as a result of how we feel about a particular situation. However, unlike values, attitudes and feelings, it is the one layer of the onion that we can actually control. For example, we may feel very angry about a situation and yet be able to behave in a calm and reasonable manner. Chapter 6, *Influencing People*, explores how you can express your feelings and yet still behave in an appropriate and constructive way.

For example:	VALUE	Boys shouldn't cry or show emotion
	ATTITUDE	Boys who cry are weak and immature
	FEELING	Uncomfortable, threatened, contemptuous
	BEHAVIOUR	Walk away or say things like 'Pull yourself together'

Remember, however, that people are different. We may have

similar values yet feel differently and subsequently behave differently to others.

- *Do not judge people by their values. We have little control over what they are.*
- *It is difficult to change either our values or those of other people. However, we can control our own behaviour and thereby influence how others* **behave**.

CYCLE OF BEHAVIOUR

If we behave in a certain way people will treat us accordingly and that will reinforce our feeling about ourselves.

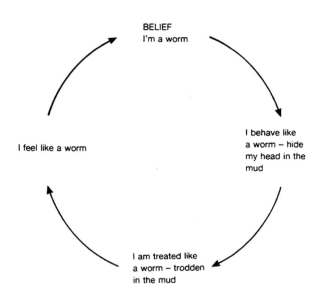

BELIEF
I'm a worm

I behave like a worm – hide my head in the mud

I am treated like a worm – trodden in the mud

I feel like a worm

To break the cycle, we need to alter our behaviour, which will begin to change the way we feel and are treated at work.

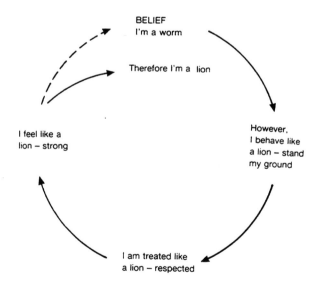

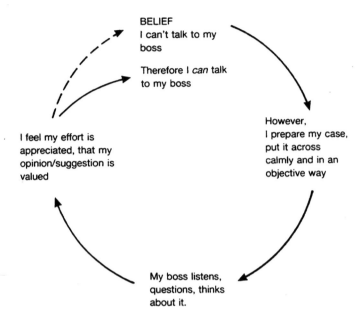

This does not work overnight or on the first occasion. If people are accustomed to treating you in a certain way because of how you behave then it will take them time to adjust to a change in your behaviour and respond accordingly. Therefore, you need to keep trying. As soon as we slip back into old behaviour patterns, people will automatically treat us in the way they have always done.

'If you always do what you have always done, you will always get what you always got.'

(*Ralph Waldo Emerson*)

FIND OUT HOW OTHERS PERCEIVE ME

Sometimes when we have behaved in a way which *we* feel to be fair and reasonable, and have not got the reaction from others that we expected or hoped for, we are surprised.

We need to be clear about the way in which we see ourselves, *and* how we are seen by others. Sometimes people see us in a very different way to the way we see ourselves.

To find out how others see us requires courage, honesty and an open mind. Sometimes the results are surprising and painful. However, it is always a valuable exercise.

- *Make a list of the people whom you consider to be your friends, colleagues who you believe respect you and people who you feel don't appear to value you very highly.*
- *Talk to these people. Find out what it is about you that they value and respect – or **dislike**.*
- *Think of a recent situation involving those people – ask them specifically about it. This is particularly useful with someone you have clashed with recently. Say things like 'I notice that you got very angry with me when we were discussing XYZ. What exactly was it about my behaviour that made you feel upset?'*
- *Ask people to give you specific examples of where your behaviour has either pleased or angered them.*
- *Try not to respond to their comments by either agreeing or disagreeing. Show that you can handle criticism by listening to what they have to say. Don't fall into the trap of trying to justify your behaviour. The objective of this exercise is to understand how people view you and why they see you in that way – not to re-open old wounds!*

It is a good idea to ask a close friend what it is about your behaviour that *they* feel may upset or irritate others – particularly if you can persuade them not to pull any punches.

Remember that people will only be honest with you if you show that you can handle it. Whether you agree or disagree with what they are saying is not the issue at this stage. Don't react – just LISTEN.

IDENTIFYING YOUR OBJECTIVES

In order to help you achieve what you want for yourself, particularly in a work context, you need to be clear about exactly what your objectives are, both in the short term, (ie, when faced with a particular situation,) and in the long term, (your ultimate goals). Think about your current job. Ask yourself the following questions:

- *What do I like about this job?*
- *What do I dislike about this job?*
- *What qualities/strengths do I bring to this job?*
- *What weaknesses do I have that make this job difficult for me?*
- *What new skills/experiences am I gaining from this job?*

This will help you establish where you are now.

The next step is to think about where you want to be. Ask yourself:

What do I want to be able to say to other people about my life when I am 75?

e.g. *'Meg O'Brennan is a valued member of the local community. She is Treasurer of the Neighbourhood Watch and organised many successful fund-raising functions to help the local schools. She was Managing Director of a large multi-national and a successful amateur artist'.*

Don't just write down what you have already achieved – imagine that you are *really* 75 and write down what you hope to have achieved by then. Then break these goals down into achievable chunks.

Objective	**Timescale**
1 *Get a professional business qualification.*	*Within next 4 years*

2   *Attend an assertiveness training course.*   *Within 6 months*

3   *Find myself a mentor.*   *Within 1 year*

4   *Look at my appearance – do I give the
     impression of being potential Managing
     Director material? Attend 'image' classes.*   *Within next 3 months*

The smaller you can break each stage into, the more likely you are to achieve your goal/objective. Make sure you set timescales against each smaller goal. When identifying your goals ask yourself WHY is it that you want to achieve them? For example, what *exactly* does Meg want to gain from being the Managing Director of a large multinational? The answer to that question may indicate whether being a Managing Director is the right route. Does Meg hope to gain the chance to influence people? Does she want the excitement of being at a senior level making policies and decisions? There are many other ways of doing that. If Meg wants to gain lots of money, then perhaps owning her own business would be a better route for her to take.

Establish what benefits you want from your goal. That knowledge will indicate whether or not your goal is realistic and how likely you are to get there.

SWOT ANALYSIS

A SWOT analysis is where you write down a list of what you have *presently* under the following headings.

Strengths	–	*eg: decisive*
Weaknesses	–	*eg: impatient*
Opportunities	–	*eg: new computer system being brought in*
Threats	–	*eg: lack of staff*

Ask a close friend or colleague to add to it or comment on it so that you are getting another perspective.

SUMMARY

- *Take action. Build on your strengths, bring them to people's attention. Look at your weaknesses, how can you address them or at the very least minimise their effect?*
- *What and where are your opportunities and threats, how can you make the most of the opportunities and minimise the threats?*
- *Always remember that people will treat you in a way that corresponds to the way in which you behave.*
- *Be positive and enthusiastic and people will listen to you. If you are negative or cynical they won't.*

MANAGING WORKLOADS AND TIME

If you want people at work, and in particular bosses, to take you seriously you need to help them feel confident and trusting in you. Only then will they value and act on your ideas and suggestions. This means you need to give the message that you are in control of your work, your emotions and your behaviour.

Focus on

- *Managing workloads and time*
- *Managing stress*
- *Managing relationships*

The simplest approach is **L I T R W**

Live In The Real World!

In the real world, things go wrong. Computers break down. People behave in ways you don't expect. Paperwork is delayed. Trains run late. Bosses are unreasonable and impatient. Accept that there are certain things that you can't change. HOWEVER, what you *can* do is change the way in which you handle the Real World.

You will probably recognise two different types of people at work. There are the kind who are always rushed and hassled, have paperwork overflowing in their in-trays, desks and drawers and are always complaining that they are too busy. Then there are the kind who always meet deadlines, are calm and unflurried and always have time to talk to people. The only thing they ever have overflowing is the waste paper bin!

In reality both these kinds of people usually have the same amounts of work to deal with as each other – and, of course, we *all* have the same amount of time available to us. What the second sort of people do differently to the first is *manage* and *organise themselves* effectively.

Time management and work management is purely and simply about *self-discipline*. The systems that you choose to help you are not the key thing. For example, you could spend £1,000,000 on a sophisticated computer system. It would however be a complete waste of money unless you had motivated and trained people to operate it. Or you could have a very simple system that suits the needs of your organisation with people who enjoy using it effectively. In the same way any time management system you choose is only effective if you can make it work, enjoy using it and most importantly – discipline yourself to stick to it.

Imagine your salary. At the end of each month you are paid an amount which is usually known to you in advance. You therefore know how much you can afford to spend on rent, mortgages, bills, holidays, food, clothes etc. If, in any given month, you receive an exceptionally large bill you adjust your money accordingly. You may choose not to go out to dinner for instance or not to put money away to save. You can do this because you *know* exactly what your income and expenditure is.

If however, you had absolutely no idea of how much money you were going to earn at the end of each month then you would have no idea of how much you could afford to spend on various items. The same principle applies to time.

We know *exactly* how much time we have available to us i.e., 60 minutes in an hour, 24 hours in a day, 7 days a week etc. This never ever changes and with the best will in the world you cannot make more time. What you can do however is make better use of your time.

You probably have a vague idea that some of your time is wasted with things such as telephone calls, computer/photocopiers breaking down etc, but you don't know *exactly*. However, given that you only have a certain pre-determined amount of time available to you, you can't possibly begin to be effective until you know precisely on what you are spending your time. Once you know that you can begin, just as you would with a salary, to re-budget and re-allocate your time.

Sometimes you have to take a tough self-disciplined approach with money and not buy that item that you wanted because you can't afford it. So too with time. Doing the easiest or most enjoyable thing is not necessarily time well spent.

So, just as you have your money salary and bank statement, you need to know what your time salary and time statement is – and that's where a daily time log comes in.

A daily time log is a simple record of where you have spent your time. Looking at your bank statement helps you to see where you have overspent and where we have cut back. Looking at a time log gives us the same information. Are you sticking to your time budget?

Analysing the time log or 'time statement' will highlight certain key areas where you can begin to save time. Could you plan in a coffee break, morning and afternoon for yourself? Could you do all your photocopying or faxing at the same time. Do you need to put aside some time for writing reports each month, or time for dealing with correspondence?

Once you have done the time log you will know where you are. You will know how much time you have and what you have to spend it on. You can then begin to prioritise your time and work.

Consider the following questions:

- *What is the purpose of your job? What are you expected to achieve? (Write down only your ultimate objective – e.g. 'the purpose of my job is to manage the resources in my team to maximise profits for my organisation').*
- *What do you need to do to achieve that purpose? Don't just make a list of day to day jobs. Note the specific things that you do in relation to the job. (e.g. – I have to visit member companies and write visit reports about those visits. The actual visit itself relates to achieving my organisation's purpose, but writing the visit report is simply an internal drill that I have to follow).*

The answers to the above questions are your *priorities*. When deciding in any one day what you should tackle first, remind yourself of your purpose. (e.g. – If I am short of time it is probably more important for me to actually visit a member company than to write up a visit report.)

DAILY TIME LOG

PAGE	DAY	DATE

START TIME	FINISH TIME	ACTIVITY	1	2	3	4	5	6	7
9.00	9.00	COFFEE							15
9.15	10.45	MEETING		90					
10.45	11.15	MORNING CORRESPONDENCE	10	15	5				
11.15	12.15	REPLYING TO POST	15		30				
12.15	12.40	INTERRUPTION						25	
12.40	1.05	SANDWICH							25
1.05	1.15	TELEPHONE CALL	10						15
		SUMMARY HRS			1				
		MINS	35	30	45	5	–	25	40

DAY
TOTAL

SHOWS MAJOR AREAS OF TIME USED
(Summarise Weekly For Overall Picture)

It is a good idea to summarise your job. Identify your key objectives and actions to achieve those objectives and take this summary to your boss for discussion. This will help to establish that you both have the same understanding of what your role is. It is also an opportunity to check out in an informal way how well you are doing.

PLANNING HOW TO MANAGE PRIORITIES

There are basically two categories into which our work falls, those tasks that are **REACTIVE** and those which are **PROACTIVE**. Reactive tasks are those which are a response and immediate. Proactive tasks are those that we can plan in advance.

- *Identify roughly what percentage of your working day/week you spend on each type. Clearly it varies during the year – but it's important to have a general idea. For instance, you many find that 70% of your job is reactive and 30% is proactive.*

Whatever the percentages are for you, this is your Real World. You need to *live* in it. That means being realistic about how you plan your time. Most people have a tendency to mentally plan 100% proactive work in a day and that is *never* achieved, because they haven't taken into account the things that 'go wrong' or the things that are going to take up more time than they anticipated. The answer, is to *plan* for things to go wrong. This means if your job is 70% reactive and 30% proactive you should plan for five hours of work in an eight hour day and leave three hours with nothing to do. This can be difficult to do because we all worry about not having enough to do. The fact is those three hours *will* fill up with all the unanticipated things that happen day to day. E.g. Interruptions, Crises, Absences.

Most of us have had the experience when at school or college of being given say, three weeks to do a piece of homework, and leaving it until the night before it was due in or doing it on the bus on the way in. How good was that piece of homework? Probably not nearly as good as it could have been if more time and trouble had been spent over it. How often did you sit down to do your homework the night before it was due in and discover you had the wrong questions? Or you had left the books you needed at school/college? How much sympathy did you get from the teacher – or even your school/college friends? Probably very little!

It is the same at work. If you leave things to the last minute then you must expect to find that the computer has broken down which means you miss your deadlines. Or the fact that you got interrupted because your boss needed you to do something urgent. In the Real World COMPUTERS BREAK DOWN! BOSSES INTERRUPT! Leaving things to the last minute is asking for trouble. You will get very little sympathy or understanding for missing a deadline that you had plenty of time to achieve even if you do say 'I had so many other things to do as well'. So – *don't* leave things to the last minute. At the very least don't do the work on the day that it's due. Do it the day before so that if something does go wrong you have left yourself a little bit of leeway.

DIARYING REACTIVE AND PROACTIVE TIME

The diary is one of the most underused resources you have. Most diaries look like the example below, simply used as a memory jogger for meetings, 1–1's, visiting clients etc. With diaries you commit your time to other people. It is harder to commit time for yourself.

EXAMPLE 1

MONDAY 18 JANUARY	TUESDAY 19 JANUARY
1030 Meeting	
XYZ Company	1230 Lunch – Margaret
1400 Meeting Fred	1500 Budgeting Meeting

Use your diary to make appointments with yourself. This will help you to manage your proactive and reactive time better and allow you to build in time in a realistic and workable way for things to go wrong. For example, you have a report to do that's due at Thursday lunchtime. If you choose to do the report on Tuesday you give yourself a full day spare if anything should crop up or something should go wrong. In the Ideal World the report might take you one hour to complete. In the Real World, you need to allow one and a half hours – in case of interruptions or something going wrong. In your diary make an appointment at 2pm to write the report. Don't schedule the next task until 3.30pm. This way you create more time for yourself, because if all goes well and you actually complete the report without interruptions, you will have gained half an hour in your diary to do something else with. Even if you are interrupted, you will still have achieved the task within the deadline you set yourself.

EXAMPLE 2

TUESDAY 20 FEBRUARY	WEDNESDAY 21 FEBRUARY
0900 General Correspondence	0900 General Correspondence
1000 Meeting Accounts	1000 Continue Budget
1300 Begin Budget	1130 Phone Michael Jones
1400 Write X Report	1200 Budget
1530 Meeting Meg	1300 Planning Team Meeting
	1700 Reception

Remember that given the opportunity to estimate how much time a job is going to take people will nearly always underestimate. Using a diary in this way will help you to make more sensible decisions about how to allocate time to others and also about agreeing to deadlines that you can realistically meet without affecting the rest of your work.

MANAGING DEADLINES

Imagine that you have been asked by your boss to meet a deadline. You argue and protest but eventually give way and agree to the deadline, knowing that in reality you won't be able to meet it. You may use the well known escape phrase 'I'll try' because you can't convince the boss otherwise or because it's the boss or a client and you feel you have to be seen to be co-operative and flexible. Then as you *knew* you would, you miss the deadline. What your boss will remember in three months' time is not only that you protested loudly, but that *you* missed a deadline that *you* had agreed to.

Imagine that instead of giving in, you stand your ground. You say that you cannot meet that deadline but offer an alternative. Your boss may well walk away from that meeting feeling frustrated and cross, but in three months' time they will remember that you are a person who having committed yourself to a deadline, sticks to it. Get people to agree to your alternative suggestion by always explaining *why* you can't meet the deadline. If people understand the reason they are much more likely to accept your refusal. But you must *always* offer an alternative deadline that you *can* meet.

Delete the letters ASAP from your vocabulary. Piles of paper marked ASAP are meaningless. If you have a pile of paperwork on your desk, all marked ASAP how do you know which one to deal with first? You don't. So you are likely to do the one that looks easy or interesting. When people write ASAP on a document they usually have an actual deadline in mind. How often has someone asked you to do something 'as soon as possible', and when you've said 'Will next Friday do?' they've shrieked 'Good Heavens, no! I need it by Tuesday at the latest!' Make sure that you put a 'return by' date on any document you send out. Customers and senior people will appreciate and be impressed by the fact that you have given them a deadline, particularly if you give them a reason.

For example, *'Please can you let me have this form back by 19*

November. I need it to complete the monthly returns which I can then send to Accounts by 30 November'. This actually helps *other* people to prioritise *their* work.

Never leave it to the last minute to chase someone if there is a deadline. You *know* that you haven't received it. It's likely that it hasn't been done. By chasing at the time of the deadline you are setting up a situation where *you* feel cross and the other person feels harassed. You are both likely to walk away from the encounter with negative thoughts about one another. Chase people up in advance of deadlines. You do this politely by using a phrase such as 'Just checking to see if there are any problems'. Better still, let people know in advance that you will be ringing them to see how they're getting on. Say something like 'I'll call the day before to see if there are any problems'. Very few people will be offended by that. In fact they are much more likely to welcome it.

ROLLING 'TO DO' LIST

A rolling 'to do' list is basically a diary or book which is dated. Instead of writing down a daily list of things to do, or a weekly one and moving things from one list to the other, write down what you have to do on the day on which you intend to do it. This is similar to the diary system, except that you write in the diary the *big jobs*, appointments to write reports and so on. In your rolling to do book you write the *little jobs*, e.g., phone Mercury, write to PD Carpets. This system will help you to make sensible decisions about making better use of your time. Don't have more than eight things to do in one day. You won't have time to do them all. Any additional tasks should be moved or planned for following days.

Monday 18/1	Tuesday 19/1	Wednesday 20/1	Thursday 21/1
* phone Mercury re X2948 * speak to Davy Jones * reply to Mark on new proposal	* check Lambeth mailing * pop up to Fred re Fiona	* write to PD Carpets * check report proofed	* speak to Mike re Marketing Plan * phone Jamie re budget

EVERYTHING BOOK

An everything book is an A4 hardback book that you carry around with you **everywhere**. Any thing at all that you have to write down, from notes in meetings to telephone messages or phone numbers, is all written in *one* book. This way you only have to look in one place for notes of numbers and meetings etc. You will never have to hunt through the bin for that little yellow sticky, that mysteriously became a little yellow *unsticky*!

Carry it around with you. How many times have you bumped into someone in the corridor and they've asked you to do something for them and by the time you got back to your desk you had completely forgotten all about it? With an everything book, not only do you not forget, it also looks extremely professional and impressive to be *seen* to write things down. It will also eliminate interruptions. People will have seen you write things down and will assume that you don't need to be reminded.

THE BRING FORWARD SYSTEM

A bring forward system is a concertina file, or drawer with lateral filing sections, numbered 1–31 (i.e. representing the days in the month).

You put in it any written material that you need to see appear on your desk on a given day.

For example, you sent a letter to someone on 10th and you want to check that you have received a reply by the 25th. Put a copy of the letter in the slot marked 25. You may have an agenda for a meeting that you have to attend on the 28th. You put the agenda in the slot marked 27 (a day early to give you time to prepare for the meeting).

Every day you pull out all the papers in the slot with that date (e.g. 25th). Remove all the ones for action in the current month and put the others back in until the next month.

Advantages of a bring forward system

- *Your desk should never be overflowing*
- *Your pending 'action' is all part-processed*
- *Nothing will 'appear' at the last moment*
- *Peaks and troughs will be ironed out*
- *Chase-up; reminders of all sorts – telephone calls, action promised*

TIME TO THINK PERIODS

A time to think period is the equivalent to having an office door which when closed means 'do not disturb' and when open means 'come on in and chat'.

There will be 2 things that make having uninterrupted time difficult to achieve.

- *You don't have an office – it's open plan.*
- *You have to be available to people.*

OPEN PLAN OFFICES

If you work in an open plan office, approach your colleagues and ask *them* if they would like to have two hours completely uninterrupted time each week. Their answer is almost undoubtedly going to be 'YES PLEASE!'. You make it a reciprocal arrangement. You answer each other's calls and deal with whatever can be dealt with for the other person for an agreed period of time. They do the same for you. You can come to this arrangement with members of your own team, or with other people. To make it work, make sure that you don't allow the other person to be interrupted and make it the same period of time every week. If you are going to permanently 'close' a section of your diary every week you should have some time, again *specifically*, allocated, that is 'interruptible'. Make sure that it's status-free. People will only stick to it if they think its in their own interests to do so.

BEING AVAILABLE

In the last year have you had a holiday, been to the doctor or dentist during the working day, attended meetings, visited clients, gone to the loo? During that time you were unavailable to customers, colleagues, members of staff. Did the world collapse? Was your department in total chaos? No. While you were unavailable people dealt with things on your behalf or someone took a message. Your in-tray was probably higher, but things were still ticking over. You *must* accept the fact that you are not indispensable. In fact, if you are indispensable you can wave goodbye to any chances of promotion. No-one will promote you out of a department which will collapse without you. If your aspirations involve moving upwards then make sure that people can cope when you're not there.

People will interrupt less if you tell them a time when you *are* available. Say something like '*I'm always tied up on Wednesday mornings, but Wednesday afternoons are a good time to pop in and see me*'.

You don't know who will turn up, but you can guarantee that someone probably will and plan your workload accordingly.

DEALING WITH TELEPHONE INTERRUPTIONS

Make telephone appointments. If you plan to ring someone, tell them (or whoever takes the message) the specific time you will be calling. If you get a message that says that someone will call you 'sometime this afternoon', you will just carry on as normal. You may go into other people's offices, pop to the photocopier and so on. The chances are that when the person rings you will be away from your desk. If, however, you receive a message saying that Fred Bloggs will be telephoning you at 3pm, you are more likely to be at your desk at that time. If you are asking someone to call you back, give them a specific time. They are then more likely to return your call when it's convenient for *you*. They are also more likely to actually return your call.

Learn the facilities that your telephone has to offer. For example, can you dial an extension and if it's engaged programme your phone to call you back when it becomes free? Modern telephone systems have lots of facilities to help you make better and more effective use of the telephone. Learn what they are.

If you telephone someone and they're unavailable, retain control of your time. Offer to ring *them* back at a specific time. This way *you* control when you interrupt your work and not the other person.

Use telephone message forms and encourage the people you work with to do the same. There is nothing more irritating than a yellow, grubby sticky thing stuck to your desk with a 'Fred phoned'. If people are required to fill in specific forms, the questions on the form will prompt them to take down the message correctly.

EXAMPLE

```
TELEPHONE MESSAGE

TO:                          TIME:

FROM:                        DATE:

COMPANY:                     TAKEN BY:

                             EXT:

TELEPHONE NO:

MESSAGE:


Please  ☐   Returned  ☐   Will  ☐   URGENT  ☐   When
ring        your call     ring                   available
back                      back                   . . . .
```

MOVEMENT SHEETS

If you or your team spend time out of the office, produce weekly movement sheets. Keep a copy in the office and give copies to travelling staff. This saves time for people who ring the office only to find that a colleague is out on business for the day. It is also more professional to look at a movement sheet and immediately be able to tell a caller where Meg is and when she will be back in the office. This is much better than yelling around the room 'Anyone know where Meg is today?' See example on page 28.

DEALING WITH INTERRUPTIONS

Interruptions are a big problem area. You will never be able to eliminate them entirely. Most of us don't handle interruptions correctly. We feel we have to be constantly available to people. When you are interrupted you will tend to stop what you are doing to talk to the other

person. What this means is that you spend time dealing with something you hadn't planned to deal with at that particular time. It also encourages people to continue interrupting because they know that you will respond.

Techniques

- *Tell people in advance when you are and are not available and stick to it.*
- *When people do interrupt, tell them that you can't deal with them right now. Give them the reason (e.g., 'I've got to get this report done by 3pm') and offer them an alternative time ('Come back at 3.30, I'll have time to talk to you properly then'). People will respond if they feel that you have taken their interruption seriously enough to offer them an alternative time. Ninety-nine out of every hundred interruptions can wait at least a few hours.*
- *Stand up when people 'pop in', to discourage them from hanging around.*
- *Ask colleagues to put a call through to you, when a perpetual interrupter turns up. The interrupter, seeing that you are busy, may then go away.*
- *Pick up some papers from your desk and head towards the photocopier or the fax. This sometimes gives them the hint.*
- *Indicate at the beginning of the interruption that you only have a certain amount of time available to speak to the person. Say something like 'I've only got 10 minutes to talk to you Fred, I have to pop in and see Bert at 3.30'.*
- ***The best method of all is honesty. Tell the interrupter that you are busy, what you are busy doing, that it's difficult at the moment but you would be glad to talk to them at an alternative time.***

Don't be guilty of interrupting people yourself. They will feel the same way about your interruption as you probably feel about theirs. It will encourage them to feel it's OK to interrupt you if you interrupt

WEEK COMMENCING 8TH MARCH 1993

NAME	MONDAY	TUESDAY	WEDNESDAY	THURSDAY	FRIDAY
MARY OVERTON Thames West	Keep Free	Helping Your Manager Meeting	Helping Your Manager Meeting	Keep Free	Directors' Meeting
LINDA HALL Thames West	Experienced Sec Taking Sessions	Experienced Sec Taking Sessions	In Office	Starting as Sec Taking Sessions	Starting as Sec Taking Sessions
VANESSA PHILLIPS Thames East	AM Office 1500 Bank	1030 V. Jardin 1430 In Office	In Office	Possible design survey meeting	Holiday
VAL TYLER Thames East	1130 V. Chris Ridgewell	1100 Ian Harris 1500 Budget meeting	Platform Skills	Platform Skills	Office
THERESA LEMONDE Southern	Travel to Warrington	Practical Communication Session	Practical Communication Session	Starting as a Secretary course	Office

them. Find out in advance when people are free and let them know you will be popping in to see them. At the very least, telephone first. Always save a group of things to talk to someone about so that you minimise the amount of times you interrupt.

Handling paperwork

Deal with paperwork at the same time every day, preferably first thing. Don't skim through paperwork. Deal with each piece of paper as you pick it up. If you can action the document – do it. Then file the paper or throw it away. Begin action on anything you can. Then file the document in the Bring Forward System for when you can take the next action. Read short items immediately. (i.e. no longer than two sides of A4). Plan time to read longer documents. Pass along circulation items within 24 hours, and throw away every piece of paper that you can.

SUMMARY

- *Live in the real world.*
- *Do a daily time log.*
- *Identify your key objectives and the actions you need to take to achieve them.*
- *Diary proactive and reactive time.*
- *Be realistic when setting and agreeing to deadlines.*
- *Keep a rolling 'to do' list and an 'everything' book.*
- *Use a Bring Forward System.*
- *Allocate 'Time to Think' periods.*
- *Make appointments for telephone calls.*
- *Handle each piece of paper only once.*

# MANAGING STRESS AND RELATION- SHIPS

In today's fast paced environment you need to balance a lot of different things in your life. Home, work, social events and so on.

This can create stress. If you allow yourself to exhibit overt signs of stress at work you can have an adverse effect on people's view of you, your capabilities, your competence.

What is stress? Everyone operates with demands placed on them. Constraints make it *difficult* to meet those demands. Supports *help* us meet them.

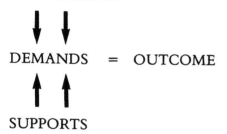

CONSTRAINTS

DEMANDS = OUTCOME

SUPPORTS

For example, your *demand* may be to meet a budget target. Your *constraint* could be a poor market because of the recession. Your *support* might be a good, committed sales team. Or the *demand* might be to have a clean home. The *constraint*, that you have to work five days a week. The *support*, a housekeeper or cleaner.

Stress basically occurs when things are out of balance. That is, when the numbers of *constraints* are greater than the *supports*. This makes it more difficult to meet the demand – creating stress. It also works in reverse. When the supports are greater than the constraints there is nothing to challenge us – creating stress.

There are five key ways to combat stress.

- *Get good time management systems in place so that stress is not caused by being disorganised.*
- *Develop awareness of your own stress levels. Identify what causes you to feel stressed.*
- *Recognise your own symptoms of stress.*
- *Build in to your lifestyle systems for coping with stress both when it occurs and as a general way of living.*
- *Be realistic – try to look at situations objectively and not over-react – and decide where you can take action or where you need to let go.*

Everyone has different stress levels. For example you may not mind a messy house, but your partner may hate it; or your boss may not be concerned about punctuality, you hate waiting.

There is no right or wrong with stress levels, simply the Real World. You have to deal with your own stress and not compare yourself to other people. It is not the level of stress, but how you deal with it that matters.

BE AWARE OF YOUR OWN STRESS LEVELS

Identify what stresses you. Write a list and give each thing a stress level rating. You can make up your own, but in the following example the rating is from 1–10 with 10 being the highest.

Late time keeping	5
Heavy workload	6
Arguments with partner	8
Car breaking down	4
Son's new girlfriend	3

This list will help you to:

- *Identify what areas you can take action on and what areas you need to let go of. (e.g., You can do something about the arguments with your partner, but you can do nothing about your son's new girlfriend so you need to let go of it.)*
- *Measure how stressed you are by your own measurements.*
- *Measure how you deal with stress and how you improve. (e.g., You may notice that something that scored 9 on your first list three months ago has become a 4 because you have developed better ways of dealing with it.)*

PERSONAL SYMPTOMS OF STRESS

Everyone exhibits different personal symptoms of stress. I have listed below the most common, but you are likely to have some that are unique to you.

PHYSICAL	*EMOTIONAL*	*BEHAVIOURAL*
tired	*feeling no one cares*	*snappy*
headaches	*erratic*	*cries a lot*
bad skin	*feeling paranoid*	
eat more	*low self esteem*	
eat less	*irritable*	
heartburn/attacks		
run down		
hyperactive		
very slow		
over/under weight		

Sudden changes in normal behaviour are good indicators of stress. If your normal behaviour is hyper-active and you suddenly become slower, you are likely to be suffering from stress. Ditto if normally slow and measured people become hyperactive.

SYSTEMS FOR COPING WITH STRESS

There are four main ways of coping with stress:

- *Tackling the problem*
- *Active Distraction*
- *Self Nurturing*
- *Emotional Expression*

TACKLING THE PROBLEM

Look at the list of things that are stressing you. Identify those things that you can take action on and those things that you can do nothing about. Write them down.

Problem	Action
Late timekeeping	*ask people to be ready 10 minutes before they need to be*
Heavy workload	*speak to boss* *delegate a job to someone else*
Arguments with partner	*what are they about?* *who is at fault?* *go out for dinner and talk*

Car breaking down	*buy a new car!!*
	get it fixed/use public transport
	allow time in the morning for problems
	accept it – can't afford to do anything about
	it this month
Son's new girlfriend	*his life, his choice, accept it.*

Don't waste a lot of time and energy trying to change things you can't. Learn when to 'let go' of something.

ACTIVE DISTRACTION

Active distraction is doing something that takes your mind off whatever it is that is stressing/worrying you. You *literally* have to concentrate on something else.

For example:	*Read*
	Watch TV
	Exercise – play a team game, play squash
	Play music

Build all of your chosen active distractions into your lifestyle. Make them habits. In this way you will help to *prevent* stress occurring as well as being able to handle it better when it does occur.

SELF NURTURING

People are good at nurturing and looking after others. They aren't as good at doing it for themselves. Treat yourself. Do things that you ordinarily might consider to be selfish. For example:

- *Lock yourself in the bathroom in a long hot bath and with a good book for an hour*

- *Buy yourself a present*
- *Treat yourself to a really nice lunch*
- *Get a cleaner*

You may feel you don't have time to relax, because you have to do the garden, clean the car, spend time with the family, and do the dishes. However, if you allow yourself to get over-stressed, the garden gets done slowly and badly. You feel even more tired. You don't clean the car properly. You are snappy with your family. You end up not nurturing yourself and not doing any of the other jobs either!

Be sensible. *LITRW*. If you don't look after and care for yourself, you won't be able to look after and care for others.

EMOTIONAL EXPRESSION

During times of extreme stress it is particularly important that you are not over independent or self-reliant. Sometimes it is difficult to see the wood for the trees. Talking to someone else can help you to put things into perspective. Bottling up emotion and always 'holding your tongue' can create more stress.

Identify your support network. Do not rely on one person alone (particularly a partner) to fill all your emotional needs. This in itself can cause stress, both for you and the other person. No one person can realistically fulfil all our needs. If you expect them to you are likely to be disappointed. Identify a person who can be:

- *Someone who you can rely on in a crisis:*

  _____

- *Someone who makes you feel good about yourself:*

  _____

- *Someone you can be totally yourself with:*

  _____

- *Someone who will tell you how well or badly you are doing:*

  _____

- *Someone to talk to if you are worried:*

  _____

- *Someone who really makes you stop and think about what you are doing:*

  _____

- *Someone who is lively to be with:*

_____

- *Someone who introduces you to new ideas, new interests, new people:*

_____

Get into the habit of sharing problems with someone you trust. Pick the right people. It is not appropriate to 'whinge' to your team.

LITRW

Live **In The Real World.** Put things into perspective. Be realistic.

If there is a problem at work that is worrying you, try to leave it there when you go home. You are unlikely to be able to do anything about it during the evening/weekend/holiday. Worrying about it tends to make the problem seem larger that it actually is.

A trick I use is to write down the things that are worrying me at work – and leave that list physically *at* work. I find that by taking the worry out of my head, putting it on a piece of paper and leaving it at work it's more likely to stay at work and allow me to concentrate on my home life.

If you are having real problems switching off, do something to actively distract yourself. You then *have* to concentrate on something other than the problem.

MANAGING RELATIONSHIPS

Relationships at work are complex.

Establish what different relationships you have with people at work. It is unlikely that you have a relationship with your boss that is as simple as that of boss and team member. You may be seen as an ally, or a foe. They may feel threatened by you. They may see you as someone who always has to be persuaded or who is easy/difficult to manage. Their perception of you will influence how successfully you communicate.

It may be that you and your boss and/or other colleagues perform functions other than your immediate job. For example, I was a Management Adviser. I was also Chair of the Union Group, a Project Leader for a Total Quality project and friends with some of the people that I worked with. That meant that whenever I was dealing with someone at work, I had to be aware of what 'hat' the other person was wearing, what role I was in or what 'hat' I was wearing, what their perception of me was.

I had to ensure that at the beginning of any conversation I clarified to the other person what hat I was wearing. As people often say 'off the record', I would say 'With my Union hat on' or 'Speaking to you as a friend'. This usually worked. Sometimes however, even when I made it clear that I was speaking as a Project Leader, people found it hard to forget that I was also Chair of the Union.

Don't expect people to automatically know which hat you are wearing. Try, particularly in meetings, to enter wearing one hat and keep that hat on for the duration. It is very confusing and unsettling for people if you keep swapping hats during a conversation or meeting unless they have specifically asked you to.

At the beginning establish which hat you are wearing, and ensure that the language and approach that you take fits the hat that you are wearing. (See Chapter 6, *Influencing People*, for more specifics on language and approach). Try to separate what people say under different hats. Take things in context. If you don't take 'tellings off' personally others will behave the same way. Show your boss and others that you understand how different relationships operate at work by responding appropriately to different situations. Don't call on a personal relationship at work for help. It is rarely appropriate. People don't forget that you've done it and you may well end up having to return the favour by doing something you don't feel happy about.

If you are down the pub on a Friday night dancing on the table, singing 'Oggy Oggy Oi' and removing your clothes, people will remember what you looked like naked across the corporate meeting table! If the boss was the one doing it, you don't need to bring it up at work. Don't forget 'Discretion is the better part of valour'.

CONFIDENTIALITY

Sometimes you hear things in confidence – business and personal matters. It is vital you don't share this with others even though it's very tempting to do so. We all have one person who we trust and they have one person they trust and they have one person they trust . . . and so it goes on. Gossip is not always malicious. It is often started by one person telling another person something in confidence.

If you don't want something to become known then don't tell *anyone* about it.

FRIENDSHIPS

Sometimes, you may form a particular friendship with a colleague or team member. This needs to be carefully managed. Clarify at the outset that at work the situation is different. Don't confide in the friend things about the rest of your team and/or the boss. No matter how conscientious and confidential the friend, the relationship will be noticed and commented on. Regardless of the true facts, people will assume favouritism and that you're telling this person things they wouldn't ordinarily know about.

Be honest with the friend. Explain the situation you are in. They will then respect and understand your situation and deal with it appropriately.

My approach to working with a team would be treat everyone as a 'friend' as well as a team member – obviously within clearly defined limits. In my experience, people respect your position more if they feel valued and trusted as individuals.

# UNDER-STANDING YOUR BOSS

Chapter 1 looked at how values are formed in childhood and how they have a major impact on attitudes, feelings and behaviour.

People have similar expectations of bosses as they do of their parents. They are expected to know all the answers, to be on 'our side', to behave in a rational adult manner all the time, never to make mistakes. When people grow up they realise that their parents are ordinary human beings like themselves and therefore make mistakes. The same is true of bosses.

As a child you probably said things like 'When I grow up and have children of my own, I am never going to treat them the way my parents treat me?' Then as a parent yourself, you find yourself thinking 'Oh my goodness, I sound just like my mother/father!' It is the same at work. I can remember wondering what my immediate manager did all day long – until I became a manager and realised that there was a lot more to the job than I had previously realised or recognised.

Although **you** may believe that your boss is useless, it is highly unlikely that your boss has the same perception of their abilities as you do.

In the diagram below which is the biggest circle?

They are both the same size. It is simply a question of perception and perspective. The circles look different sizes *because* of the different sized circles that surround them. The context is different. The same principle applies to bosses. They will seem to be different depending on the context they are in. They are the same person, but will be seen differently by their colleagues, team, family and friends.

Very few bosses believe that they are not good bosses. Most of them blame their subordinates. Just as most subordinates don't believe that they are bad subordinates, they blame the boss!

To understand the boss, you need to know certain things about them:

- *Their career history*
- *Their career future – both what they aspire to and what is likely.*
- *Their objective for their current job – what do they actually do.*
- *Their problems/difficulties with the current job.*
- *Their relationship with their boss/es.*
- *How they see their relationship with you.*

CAREER HISTORY

People are influenced by what has happened to them in their past. Your perception of the world of work is based on what your personal experience has been. For example, if your boss worked for a very hierarchical, autocratic organisation in the past they will have picked up some of those management techniques and may approach managing you in a similar style. Even though that style isn't appropriate, that is the style they learned. They will use it, often without realising that they are.

How 'well' has your boss done career-wise? Has it taken a long time to get to the top? Were they frequently 'passed over'? Has their career trajectory been meteoric and they plan to move onwards and upwards with equal rapidity?

How long has your boss been in the current job? What kinds of changes have they had to deal with and over what period of time? The answers to these questions will give you a better picture of your boss.

CAREER FUTURE

All of us have aspirations. Those aspirations are not necessarily to do with moving further up the management ladder. Sometimes a boss's aspiration is simply to stay where they are and be successful and well respected. Or they may wish to move into a different field of work altogether. Find out what your boss wants to do with their career. This will influence their behaviour towards you, their colleagues and their bosses. Just as our bosses can affect your career, so too can you affect theirs, both by actively helping them to further it or simply by being a good team member. You will know your organisation. How well is your boss thought of? How likely do you think it is that they will get promotion if they want it? Think what you can do to help your boss in their career plans. It's a two-way process. If you want your boss to help develop you, you need to see what you can do to help them.

If you have a strong enough relationship with your boss then perhaps you could talk openly and honestly with them about their career plans.

Many organisations are now introducing 'Upward Appraisal'. Team members are encouraged to give their boss open, honest and constructive feedback about their strengths and weaknesses as managers. Try to build up the kind of relationship with your boss where you can give them this kind of feedback. Remember that often bosses don't realise that they are making mistakes with the team – usually because no-one in the team has ever told them.

THE HILL, THE HIGH GROUND, THE HORIZON

Every manager at varying stages of their career fits into one of the following categories:

The Hill	**Junior/Middle Management**
The High Ground	**1st General Manager level job**
The Horizon	**Director Level**

At each level they will be concentrating on different things, and the level that they are at will generally influence their approach to the job.

THE HILL

If your boss is at this level, they are probably quite close to the ground level workings of the organisation. They will have a very specific remit, specific budgets and a lot of day to day operational duties. Because there are probably several layers above them they are less likely to be able to influence policy and direction. This may mean that they are less able to be flexible in the way they manage their part of the organisation. They will be expected to implement other people's policies and rules. They are unlikely to be involved very much in the decision making process. They may find themselves having to implement decisions that they don't necessarily understand or agree with. They may feel torn between loyalty to the team and loyalty to their boss. Ultimately, their loyalty as managers *must* be to the organisation.

THE HIGH GROUND

At this level the manager will be slightly remote from the workings of front line staff. They will probably have access to some of the decision-making process. They are likely to have several layers of management underneath them. They will have responsibility and accountability for a larger part of the organisation and specific budgets to work to. They will be concerned more with monthly performance than daily. Their key responsibility will be to get other people to achieve budgets. They are also more likely to have had an input into what those budgets are. They will need to have an overview of several different teams and will spend quite a lot of time planning. They will have more opportunities to influence the direction of the organisation as a whole.

THE HORIZON

Managers at this level are likely to be Directors or above. They are probably remote from the ground-level workings of the organisation and will rely heavily on feedback from managers at lower levels. They will have a key responsibility for setting the aims and objectives of the organisation and for strategic planning (i.e. looking 5+ years ahead). They will probably feel they have the freedom to be flexible in organising and managing themselves and their teams. They will need to rely heavily on others for implementation of policies. They will therefore spend a lot of time in meetings and face to face discussions. They will expect to be given information without having to ask for it. They will have a bigger overview of the organisation as a whole and be expected to see a wider picture than simply the part they are accountable for. They will be expected to be thinking and planning on a yearly/three yearly/long term basis.

THEIR OBJECTIVE FOR THE CURRENT JOB . . .
OR WHAT DO THEY ACTUALLY DO WITH THEIR TIME?

You need to know how your boss spends their time. You can establish this by simply asking them. This will show your boss that you are interested. It will also ensure that when they're not available you will be able to provide a more effective back-up. Find out:

- *What are they measured on by **their** boss?*
- *How much of their time do they spend*
  problem-solving
  planning
  routine, daily tasks
  meeting customers
  meetings generally
  financial – e.g. budgeting monthly accounts
- *Of that time, which tasks are their priorities?*
- *Which of their tasks do you have direct input or influence over?*

Find out what they actually want to accomplish with *this* job. Do they simply want to meet the budget? Or keep the department ticking over? Do they want to make a big impact, introduce radical changes? Knowing this will help you to understand why your boss behaves/responds in certain ways.

Be realistic – your boss is the one who is accountable overall for results. By being obstructive you create a situation where neither of you is effective, or seen to be. If you don't agree with what your boss is doing in this job then take appropriate action as follows:

- *Present your objections clearly, calmly and factually – no vague generalisations. Give facts.*
- *Give coherent, well researched and well thought out arguments and reasons for your objections.*
- *Offer alternative suggestions/solutions.*
- *If your boss still feels that the actions they are taking are the right ones then you must support them.*
- *If the boss makes a mistake, avoid saying 'I told you so'.*

THEIR PROBLEMS

For most people, the job that we do is not always easy and enjoyable. Every job brings with it difficulties and problems which need to be solved or dealt with in some way. Generally speaking the problems fall into three main areas:

- *Technical*
- *People*
- *Financial/budgetary*

TECHNICAL

Technical problems will tend to be influenced by budgetary requirements. For instance, a particular piece of equipment or machinery isn't really up to the job but there is no money available with which to replace it. This means that the boss will have a lot of pressure put on them by the people who have to operate that particular piece of equipment, or by other managers/departments whose work is influenced by it. Senior managers will expect them to make the best of what is available.

Your boss will be looking for as much support and help as possible from you. They will need regular feedback, creative ideas and suggestions from you and your team and they will particularly need you to keep your team motivated. If the money isn't available (which is very often the case) then they will need you to help them make this understood and accepted by others.

Never go into your boss with a whinge about technical problems. To be effective you need to make sure that you take in with your 'whinge' some ideas and suggestions as to how the difficulty might be overcome.

PEOPLE

People problems generally occur due to a lack of understanding and communication.

For your boss this may be an area that causes the most worry. The 'people' problems might be with his/her boss, peers or even with their own team. Nine out of ten 'people' problems can be overcome by ensuring that you are dealing with facts and not emotions. Make sure that you have supplied your boss with facts when they are dealing with a 'difficult' person.

It may be that the boss themself has what we often call 'an unfortunate manner'. This means they antagonise people in the way they approach and speak to them. Often the boss will be completely unaware of this because it will be unlikely that anyone has ever pointed it out.

If you don't have the kind of relationship with your boss where you can tell them what appears to be going wrong in their dealings with people, can you approach someone else whom the boss will listen to? The secretary may be able to help. Many bosses rely quite heavily on a secretary for that kind of feedback. Or perhaps the Personnel Department, if you have a dedicated resource. They are usually fairly independent and may be in a better position to point out the problem areas.

FINANCIAL/BUDGETARY

Your boss is measured on how well they stick to the budgetary constraints they have, both in terms of expenditure and income. This will place a lot of stress on your boss, particularly when they are relying heavily on other people to stick to those budgets.

ACTION BY YOU

- *At budgeting time prepare your information well in advance. Be specific and realistic about your expenditure needs and/or your income generating targets.*
- *Keep them up-dated on current and likely future performance.*
- *Inform them immediately it appears that there may be a problem.*
- *Get your own team to understand and 'own' the budget. They will then be budget conscious and more likely to stick to it.*
- *Have soundly researched arguments ready if you need to overspend the budget.*

THEIR RELATIONSHIP WITH THEIR BOSS

For most people at work, the most important relationship that they have is with their boss. Bosses can be the biggest influence on our working lives. They can help or hinder our career prospects, how much money we earn and how well or badly we are enabled to do our job. This can be as true of very senior people as it is of us. Your boss's relationship with his or her boss will have a big impact on how they approach their job. You need to know what this relationship is. Does your boss's boss keep a very close eye on what's going on? Are they very remote? Do they give your boss a free hand or are there tight controls in place? If your boss is being tightly and closely managed and expected to be able to answer questions on every detail of their operation that is how they will manage you. Not necessarily through choice, but because they have little other option because of the way in which they are being managed.

If your boss is given a free hand then they are more likely to give you freedom in the way you do your job, manage your team, your budget. People at work are measured by their bosses on results. However some boss's bosses also measure the way in which those results are achieved.

Never forget that if you or your team 'mess up' the person who gets it 'in the neck' is your boss. Understanding the way in which your boss is managed by their boss will help you anticipate the demands your boss places on you.

HOW THEY SEE THEIR RELATIONSHIP WITH YOU

How does your boss see you? Do you know or do you make assumptions about it?

You probably consider yourself to be a 'good' worker, someone who achieves. Yet when bosses get together you often hear them commenting on how some of their team are whingers, inefficient, ineffective, difficult to get on with or unco-operative.

There are two main reasons for a poor working relationship with your boss.

- *Not understanding your boss.*
- *Not knowing the way in which your boss sees you.*

To identify how your boss sees you look for clues in their behaviour towards you. It is better to just *ask* them how they see you. If you do ask directly however, don't fall into the trap of either justifying yourself or feeling misunderstood. Their perception of you is as true as someone else's perception of you which may be quite different. You can only change that perception by changing or adjusting your behaviour.

- *If your boss gets impatient with you it may be that you have been doing too much whinging or that they feel your complaints are unconstructive.*
- *If your boss reacts aggressively towards you it may be that you have behaved in an aggressive manner yourself or responded to them in kind.*
- *Does your boss actively seek out your views and opinions? If they don't it may be because you have not responded positively and supportively in the past.*
- *Do they avoid spending time talking with you/your team? This may mean that they don't feel welcomed or appreciated. They may feel isolated when they come to your area of work.*

Are you seen to be co-operative, helpful, effective, understanding, supportive, interested, keen to achieve, able and willing to solve problems? Or are you seen as unco-operative, a whinger, unsupportive, disloyal (ie, complaining openly about them to your team or other people in the organisation)? If it's the latter, the only way you will change that perception is by adjusting your behaviour.

You may sometimes feel justified in having a general whinge about the boss. Imagine how *you* would feel if you were to hear someone in your team or one of your colleagues saying the things about you to others that you say about your boss to them.

THE SECRETARY

If your boss has a secretary, develop a good working relationship with her/him.

A secretary is key to any boss. They are rarely 'just' typists – they are likely to have a good understanding of the different pressures and the heaviness of the boss's workload. Find out from the secretary the best time to approach the boss, and the best method to use. The secretary will usually know what the boss finds irritating or constructive, what they are likely to respond to or reject.

SUMMARY

- *See your boss in perspective.*
- *Get to know how they spend their time and what their aspirations are.*
- *Present your ideas clearly, unemotionally and factually.*
- *Identify possible solutions to problems.*
- *Find out what your boss's perception of you is.*
- *Be loyal.*

GETTING YOUR POINT ACROSS

In the world of work you have many opportunities in which to be heard and noticed. Every form of communication you undertake will be helping people to formulate opinions about you. The letters you send, the meetings you attend or being over-heard chatting to someone in the corridor or on the telephone. It is really important that you get your communication right.

WRITTEN COMMUNICATION

LETTERS, MEMOS AND REPORTS

When beginning a piece of written communication think about your objective and consider what language and approach is going to help you to achieve that objective. This means a radical re-thinking of the language you use. Traditional 'business-speak' in both letters and memos is no longer considered to be appropriate. In today's world you must ensure that people clearly understand and therefore act on your communication. That means using simple, every day language. You must get across all the things that you need to, without clouding your messages with irrelevant or ambiguous extra information.

PLANNING YOUR COMMUNICATION

With written communication the key to success is proper planning and preparation. Organise your thoughts and the information you have available to you in a way that will help you to put across a clear, concise, structured and relevant message by using a pattern note.

PATTERN NOTES

For centuries, people have organised information in vertical lists or sentences. It was popularly believed that the brain naturally arranged spoken and written material in linear forms. However, new research has shown that the brain is continually analysing, interpreting and juggling whole inter-related networks of thoughts and ideas. Pattern notes enable the brain to relate to information more naturally and efficiently.

HOW ARE PATTERN NOTES MADE?

- *Take a plain sheet of paper and write the main theme in the centre.*
- *Using capital letters, write down all the ideas and thoughts you have on the subject, starting from the circle and branching out along lines of connecting ideas.*
- *Let your mind be as free as possible. Do not restrict your thoughts by deciding where each point should go in a list. Your ideas should flow easily.*
- *When finished, circle any related ideas and sections and establish your order of priorities and organisation.*

EXAMPLE

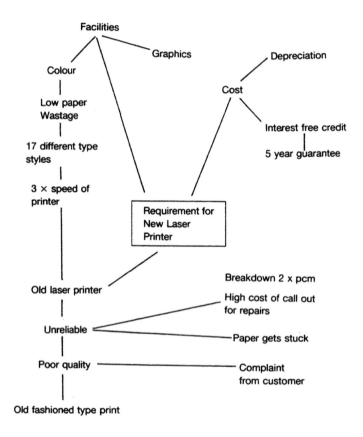

Ask someone else to look at your pattern note and add to it anything they think you may have missed. Now put all the information on your pattern note into a form that is easily understood.

LETTERS AND MEMORANDA

Keep a letter or memo short, ideally one side of A4 maximum. The more senior the person to whom you are sending the letter or memo, the less likely they are to have time to read it.

- *Keep it short and to the point.*
- *Avoid lengthy paragraphs.*

If the correspondence is asking for something or asking someone to do something, think about their 'handle'. That is whatever it is that is of interest to *them* rather than to you. For example, you may want a new laser printer for your department, and in order to get it you need approval from a number of different people. Think about the particular interests of those individuals and angle the tone of your letter accordingly. 'Angle to their handle'!

The Finance Director will be primarily interested in the cost implications. The Marketing Director will be interested in the corporate image and the professional look. The simple rules are:

Think about the reader:
- *Who is it*
- *What are their concerns/interests?*
- *What are they likely to be looking for?*
- *What language/jargon do they use?*
- *What benefit to them is there in your request/suggestion?*

MEMORANDUM

To: Cathy Jones, Finance Director
From: Lesley Smith, Head of R & D
Date: 24 July 1992

LASER PRINTER FOR R & D DEPARTMENT

Cathy,
I have identified a need for a new laser printer for our department. The old one is not presently adequate for our needs.

OLD PRINTER

- *Breakdown on average twice a month.*
- *Call out for repairs costs £65 each time.*
- *Paper continually gets stuck. We waste an average 20 sheets per every 100 at a cost of 75p per sheet.*

NEW PRINTER

- *Price £2572*
- *5 year guarantee*
- *Wastage 1 sheet per 1000 sheets*
- *Depreciation – 1000 p.a. over 2½ years*
- *Interest free credit.*

I attach the brochure giving more information about the printer. Please can you sign the necessary authorisation.
Many thanks.
Lesley

MEMORANDUM

To: Michael Martin, Marketing Director
From: Lesley Smith, Head of R & D
Date: 24 July 1992

LASER PRINTER FOR R & D DEPARTMENT

Michael,

I have identified a need for a new laser printer for my department. The old one has been giving us the following problems:

- *Old fashioned type-print*
- *Frequently breaks down*
- *Printed quality not very good (see attached example)*
- *The comment was made by a customer that the quality of our printed reports did not match the professional, up-to-date image we are trying to project.*

NEW LASER PRINTER

- *Has 17 different type styles*
- *Can print in 4 different colours*
- *Can do graphics*
- *Can print documents at 3 times the speed of the old one*

I attach a brochure giving more information about the printer. Please can you sign the necessary authorisation.
Many thanks.
Lesley

REPORTS

Lengthy reports are rarely properly read. Most people simply read the summary and the recommendations. Therefore put your efforts into making these simple and easy to read.

Winston Churchill said 'Do not let your report become a monument to your knowledge'. In other words, make sure that you only include the information that is necessary.

WRITING THE REPORT

- *Set aside quiet time*
- *Structure:*   *title page*
  contents
  summary
  introduction
  findings
  conclusions
  recommendations
  appendices
  acknowledgements/
  references
  index

LANGUAGE

Do not use over-formal language. Use the word that most accurately reflects what it is you mean. For example:

Instead of **Request**   use **Ask**
Instead of **Terminate**   use **End**
Instead of **Purchase**   use **Buy**

The same is true for phrases. For example:

Instead of **Please do not hesitate to**   use **Please**
Instead of **At this moment in time**   use **Now**
Instead of **Endeavour to ascertain**   use **Try to find out**

Avoid using phrases like 'try to', 'attempt to', 'maybe' etc. These do not leave the reader with a feeling of confidence and trust. Be positive and punchy, and use the word 'I' rather than 'The Company' or 'The Department'. It is always better to say:

'I will find out where the missing payment came from' than *'The department will endeavour to ascertain where the missing payment emanated from and inform you accordingly'*.

Avoid words that sound 'blaming'. For instance it is better to say:

'There appears to be a misunderstanding' or *'I have not received a reply'* than it is to say *'You have not understood'* or *'You failed to reply'*.

If the reader feels that you are putting them at fault, by placing the blame on them, they are less likely to respond in a positive way to your request for action.

WRITING CHECKLIST

Do

- *Keep in mind your objective*
- *Think about what will interest the reader*
- *Check what form of address (ie. Sir/ Madam/John etc.) they are comfortable with*
- *Check the spelling of their name and job title*

Don't

- *Use old-fashioned phrases like 'please do not hesitate to contact us*
- *Have long sentences and paragraphs*

- *Keep the letter/memo short*
- *Have a heading*
- *End with your action/their action*
- *Check out the house-style for your organisation.*

TELEPHONES

The telephone is the most public and noted form of communication. Because the person at the other end of the telephone cannot see you it is particularly important that you ensure that you are clearly heard. But above all, you must *listen*.

People usually see the telephone as an interruption to their 'real' work. The fact is that for most of us the telephone actually represents our 'real' work – it might be a customer (either internal or external).

See the telephone as a tool that *helps* you to do your jobs.

CHECKLIST FOR USING THE TELEPHONE

Do
- *Answer with your name (and if necessary your department)*
- *Be clear in advance about what you want to achieve as a result of the telephone call*
- *Have the relevant file to hand*
- *Think about the timing of a call (anytime between 12–2pm or after 4pm on a Friday will probably be largely unproductive)*
- *Offer/agree to take messages*
- *Follow up and check that the promised action has been taken*
- *Make notes of the conversation*

- *Answer the phone promptly (3–5 rings is acceptable – if the phone rings for any longer than that it looks unprofessional).*

Don't
- *Eat, drink, smoke on the phone*
- *Be evasive*
- *Be negative*
- *Hold two conversations at once*
- *Assume that the other person has the time to listen to you there and then*
- *Use jargon*
- *Transfer people around the organisation*
- *Sound reluctant to take a message*
- *Forget to pass on messages*
- *Interrupt*

MEETINGS

The way you handle yourself at meetings is very public and visible because it's the one forum where lots of people can actually see you in action. Whether the meeting is large and formal or small and informal your performance will be noticed. As with most other forms of communication the key to success here is preparation.

PREPARATION

Sometimes you will be summoned to a meeting where you haven't been issued in advance with a formal agenda. This is *not* an excuse for not preparing. Ring up whoever called the meeting. Either ask for an agenda or whether there is anything you can prepare in advance. This will do two things:

- *Ensure that you are prepared and have some idea of what is to be covered at the meeting*
- *Impress the person holding the meeting because you've shown some initiative.*

If there is an agenda – do go through each item on it do any preparation needed. If in doubt, telephone the person who put the item on the agenda and ask them directly what they expect you to prepare. If there is a particular item that you wish either to raise at the meeting or put on the agenda, do the following:

- *Be sure of your facts. Talk in specifics not generalities. Give examples.*
- *Be prepared for objections/criticisms. Anticipate what they might be and be prepared to deal with them unemotionally and constructively.*
- *Identify the strongest points in your arguments and concentrate on them. You are more likely to win your case on two or three arguments that are well researched and of a good quality than on lots of poorly prepared, emotional arguments.*

DURING THE MEETING

- *Arrive five minutes early.*
- *Bring with you the agenda, minutes of the last meeting and your preparation notes.*
- *Don't interrupt the speakers: indicate your desire to speak by putting your hand up. (This may be reminiscent of school days – but it's much more polite and effective).*
- *If you're unclear on a point ask the speaker or Chair to summarise for you.*
- *Clarify actions. Too many meetings end with 'someone will do that when they can' which actually 'results' in no result! Ask 'who will be doing what and by when?'*

- *Respect other people's views – even if they don't match you own. Don't say –*
  'That's a load of rubbish'
  Say – 'I see that's your view. However, my view is that . . .'.
- *During the meeting jot down on paper the points you want to make – this will:*
  - *prevent you interrupting*
  - *help you stick to the point*
  - *help you to remember the key points you want to make.*
- *Do listen to what people are saying, – avoid assuming you know what the other person wants or is really saying. The only way you can know what they really mean is either by listening or asking – **preferably both**.*
- *Make a note yourself of any actions you are asked to take and the deadlines.*
- *Don't be afraid to ask the obvious or stupid questions. Most of the time, if **you** are unclear it is likely that other people are too. (How many meetings have you been to where someone else asked the 'stupid' question and you heaved a sigh of relief because you were unclear too?) There is actually no such thing as a stupid question. Any question asked means that someone doesn't know the answer – that's not stupid. The stupid thing to do is not ask the question at all.*

Confucius said 'She/he who asks a question is a fool for a moment, she/he who never asks a question is a fool for life'. If you don't ask the question and get the answer you are likely to do the wrong thing and look even more foolish. Has anyone ever said to you 'Well, why didn't you ask?' Avoid that by making sure that you do.

AFTER THE MEETING

Do what you agreed to do at the meeting. Leave time immediately after the meeting to take or begin any action you agreed to.

You may worry that because you have a reputation for getting things done you will get lumbered with even more to do. However, a

reputation for delivering what you promised is a good thing and it puts you in a stronger position to clearly and justifiably say no to some things.

SUCCESSFUL PRESENTATIONS

PREPARATION

- *Use a pattern note to plan what you want to say in your presentation.*

- *Be clear of your objective. What do you actually want people to do? Decide what action you want them to take and focus on it.*
- *Structure the presentation so that it logically leads up to the action that you want people to take.*
- *As with written communication, use simple clear language, avoiding jargon.*
- *Always angle your presentation towards the interests of the people listening — your audience. (Angle to the handle.) If the audience is diverse, try to include a sentence or two in the presentation that will catch the attention of people with different interests.*
- *Anticipate objections and questions. Deal with the most obvious ones in the body of the presentation.*
- *Prepare flip charts or overheads in advance. Handwriting on flipchart is acceptable. Never use handwritten overheads. If you can't have overheads produced properly, then don't use them at all.*
- *When using the flipchart use at least four different colours. A flipchart written all in one colour is visually uninteresting.*
- *Avoid reading a script. Write out your presentation in full and then copy the key words on to speakers cards as in the example below. When you read from your speech cards the presentation will then sound natural and will 'flow' better. Remember to number your cards and tie them together.*

FOR EXAMPLE: CARDS

- Time Management = Self Discipline   (4)
- Salary – Time Logs
- Proactive/Reactive Time

- Using Diary (draw on f/chart)   (5)
- Rolling 'to do' list
- B/F System
- Summarise: Do what works for you

GIVING THE PRESENTATION

- *Always stand up – this gives authority to what you are planning to say.*
- *Make sure you don't fiddle with anything, eg. earrings, pens, money in pockets etc.*
- *Look at people as you are talking to them. (I remember at school assemblies our headmistress, who found public speaking somewhat nerve wracking, always used to look over our heads – in the general direction of heaven. Accordingly we all presumed that she was talking to the angels and not to us and subsequently paid no attention to what she was saying.) If you don't maintain eye contact with people, regardless of how riveting the subject matter, they will soon lose interest.*
- *Speak slowly and clearly and emphasise key words with a change of tone of voice.*
- *REMEMBER whenever you are giving a presentation your audience almost invariably **want** you to succeed. They are on your side because they want to find it interesting. People are not actually trying to catch you out, they want you to get it right.*
- *Make it clear at the beginning whether people can interrupt with questions. Generally speaking, I find it more effective to ask people to jot down any questions they wish to ask as they go along and then ask them at the end. Unless you are particularly skilful, the danger in allowing people to interrupt*

with questions is that you get side tracked and lose the point – and of course questions often beget questions.

- *Thank people at the end for listening. To have people listen to us is not our right – it is something we earn.*

SUMMARY

- *Prepare thoroughly for all communication.*
- *Keep in mind the interests of the reader or audience – 'Angle to the handle'.*
- *Be brief and to the point.*
- *Avoid jargon or technical terms.*

# INFLUENCING PEOPLE

Our behaviour influences people's view of us, their behaviour and their actions. Position, authority and status do not give us the right for people to treat us in a certain way. We earn that right by the way in which we behave towards them.

TRANSACTIONAL ANALYSIS

Transactional Analysis (TA) is a way of analysing how people speak to and behave towards one another.

In Chapter 1 we mentioned how we have little control over the values we acquire as children. This also applies to the 'ego states' of TA.

An ego state is something that we think/feel at any given point in time and how we therefore relate to other people.

In TA there are basically six ego states, three of which are effective and healthy – in other words they get us what we want and help us deal effectively with other people. The other three are ineffective and when used are likely to lead to breakdowns in communication and relationships with people at work and at home.

Everyone has all six ego states – but some of them are used more by some people than others. People change ego states relatively readily, generally in response to the behaviour of others around them.

In a face-to-face communication, knowing what ego state you and the other person in will help you to adjust your behaviour and speech to get a satisfactory outcome. You want to feel OK about yourself. The other person wants to feel OK about themselves.

The six ego states are:

EFFECTIVE EGO STATES   *INEFFECTIVE EGO STATES*

(NP)   *Nurturing Parent*   (CP)   *Critical Parent*

(A)   *Adult*   (RC)   *Rebellious Child*

(NC)   *Natural Child*   (CC)   *Complaint Child*

The words *Parent*, *Adult* and *Child* are used because they effectively describe the behaviours. For example, *Parents* look after you/tell you off/correct you; *Adults* listen calmly and rationally, evaluate information and make decisions based on facts; *Children* are creative, curious, fun, naughty, etc.

EFFECTIVE EGO STATES

1. NATURAL CHILD

Natural Child (NC) behaviours are about having needs and wants either met or not met and responding accordingly – that is in an open, honest and non-manipulative way.

In an NC state, if I ask for something to be done and it gets done I am pleased and will show my appreciation and gratitude openly and honestly. If it is not done and I feel angry I will show my anger in the same way. Anybody dealing with or communicating with me will know exactly what I am feeling by my behaviour and the words I use.

Behaviour

- *Spontaneous*
- *Open*
- *Honest*
- *Open minded*
- *Creative*
- *Enthusiastic*

Words

- *I*
- *Feel*
- *Happy*
- *Angry*
- *Need*
- *Want*

2. ADULT

The **Adult** ego state behaviours are about analysing and evaluating information and making decisions and balanced judgements about things.

The **Adult** ego state deals with facts not emotions, data, not feelings. The **Adult** ego state responds to the feelings and emotions of its **Natural Child** ego state and **Parent** ego state by thinking before speaking. Trying to understand why it is about to respond or behave in a particular way and making a conscious choice.

Behaviour

- *Calm*
- *Rational*
- *Analytical*
- *Unemotional*
- *Logical*
- *Reasonable*

Words

- *Why?*
- *When?*
- *Where?*
- *What?*
- *How?*
- *Does it make sense?*
- *Accurate*
- *Outcome/result*

3. NURTURING PARENT

The **Child** ego state is about **I**. The **Adult** ego state is about **it**. The **Parent** ego state is about **you**.

When in a **Parent** ego state you are **literally** behaving the way your parents behaved.

For example, parents look after you, feed you, comfort you, smack you, dismiss you, tell you off, set examples.

The **Nurturing Parent** is the ego state that is primarily concerned with looking after, nurturing and comforting people. It is understanding and tries to make people feel good about themselves by instilling confidence. It tells you when your behaviour is OK or not OK in a way that still allows you to feel good about yourself.

Behaviour

- *Caring*
- *Understanding*
- *Listens*
- *Supportive*
- *Available*

Words

- *It's alright*
- *Don't worry*
- *Everybody makes mistakes*
- *If you do X, Y will happen*
- *You're OK/important*
- *I like/love/value you*

These are the effective ego states and when operating out of these you will usually succeed in getting your needs and wants met.

INEFFECTIVE EGO STATES

1. REBELLIOUS CHILD

The **Natural Child** state is spontaneous and pro-active. The **Rebellious Child** ego state (and incidentally the **Compliant Child**) is reactive. It results as a response to the behaviour of others. The **Rebellious Child** rebels even if what is being asked of it is reasonable and makes sense. The **Rebellious Child** doesn't believe that the person it is communicating with is OK and therefore on principle it refuses to comply.

Behaviour

- *Slouches*
- *Doesn't listen*
- *Interrupts*
- *Angry*

Words

- *Why should I?*
- *What gives you the right to tell me what to do?*
- *It's not fair*
- *No, I won't*

2. COMPLIANT CHILD

In **Compliant Child** you do what other people want you to do regardless of how you feel about it. You behave in the way you believe other people expect/want you to behave rather than in the way that more appropriately matches how you feel (as you would in **Natural Child**). Even if common sense tell you not to comply with the request – you still do.

Behaviour

- *Quiet*
- *Whining*
- *No eye contact*
- *Slow*

Words

- *If I have to*
- *Oh, alright then*
- *Nobody listens to/cares about me*
- *What's the point?*

3. CRITICAL PARENT

The **Critical Parent** ego state is about blaming others and giving unconstructive criticism. The **Critical Parent** attacks other people, doesn't listen. isn't interested in explanation, is extremely judgmental.

Whereas the **Nurturing Parent** will say 'I like you, I don't like the way you behaved', the **Critical Parent** will say 'What you did proves you're an awful person.'

The **Critical Parent** writes off 'you' as a person rather than dealing with your behaviour.

Behaviour

- *Angry*
- *Critical*
- *Aggressive*
- *Sarcastic*
- *Judgmental*
- *Doesn't listen*

Words

- *Should/shouldn't*
- *Always*
- *Incapable*
- *Totally wrong*
- *Totally right*

We all use these ego states and communicate with people who also use those ego states. Recognise what ego state the other person is in and respond accordingly. For example, if a person is in *Critical Parent* they will communicate more effectively with you if you use your *Adult* ego state. For instance, when they say 'always' you say ' when, specifically?'

INTERPERSONAL SKILLS

The term 'interpersonal skills' means choosing the appropriate behaviour to achieve the best outcome for all parties in a communication.

There are several different kinds of behaviour you encounter when dealing with people. Chapter 1 talked about how people behave in certain ways because of their values (given to them as children), their attitudes/beliefs and their feelings. Through interpersonal skills you attempt to take these things into account.

People behave in particular ways because as children they learned that they could get what we call 'pay offs'. Exhibiting a certain kind of behaviour meant that they got what they wanted. Unfortunately, as children we could usually only see things in the short term and couldn't appreciate that although our behaviour might pay us dividends in the short term, in the long term it was likely to create more problems for us.

The three main types of behaviour we learned as children are AGGRESSIVE, PASSIVE and MANIPULATIVE.

AGGRESSIVE behaviour is behaving in a way that means we get what we want but at the expense of another person's feelings, wants and needs. PASSIVE behaviour is behaving in a way that means we end up doing what someone else wants, regardless of our own feelings, wants and needs. MANIPULATIVE behaviour is behaving in a way that gets us what we want by putting the other person in a position where they would feel guilty or bad if they didn't do what we wanted. In effect, manipulative behaviour is actually aggressive behaviour, well disguised!

CHARACTERISTICS OF AGGRESSIVE BEHAVIOUR

- *Doesn't listen to others*
- *Shouts/raises voice*
- *Loses temper*
- *Says 'I' not 'you' or 'we'*
- *Refuses to back down*
- *Refuses to compromise*
- *Gets own way*

PAYOFFS OF AGGRESSIVE BEHAVIOUR

- *Gets own way*
- *Not argued with in future*
- *Feels in control*
- *Feels in charge*
- *Feels listened to and obeyed*

LONG TERM PROBLEMS OF AGGRESSIVE BEHAVIOUR

- *People don't consult you, ask for your advice*
- *'Obedience' to your request/command is short term*
- *People feel defensive, resentful, frustrated*
- *People won't tell you the truth because they're afraid of your reaction*

CHARACTERISTICS OF PASSIVE BEHAVIOUR

- *Doesn't listen to others*
- *Doesn't say what they want*
- *Quiet, doesn't speak out, particularly in public*
- *Does things resentfully*
- *Says 'you' rather than 'I' or 'we'*
- *Complains and whines a lot*
- *Acts the martyr*
- *Doesn't get own way*

PAYOFFS OF PASSIVE BEHAVIOUR

- *Not bothered*
- *Doesn't have to think or come up with solutions*
- *Gets left alone*

LONG TERM PROBLEMS OF PASSIVE BEHAVIOUR

- *People don't consult you or ask for your views*
- *People feel exasperated and resentful*
- *People feel guilty and frustrated*
- *You end up doing things you don't want to do or don't agree with*

CHARACTERISTICS OF MANIPULATIVE BEHAVIOUR

- *Sulks*
- *Sarcastic*
- *Doesn't come straight to the point*
- *Plays on people's feelings, particularly of guilt*
- *Gets own way*

PAYOFFS OF MANIPULATIVE BEHAVIOUR

- *Gets own way*
- *Feels in control*

LONG TERM PROBLEMS OF MANIPULATIVE BEHAVIOUR

- *People feel confused, angry, guilty*
- *You are not believed or trusted*
- *People are reluctant to approach you/ask for advice*

DEFAULT BEHAVIOUR

Everyone exhibits behaviours along an axis, particularly when faced with possible conflict.

Passive ——————————————————————— Aggressive
                              |
                    Manipulative

Human beings react like computers. A computer programme has a 'default' setting. In other words, when you switch it on it will have a particular margin setting and command menu. You can then change the menu or the margin while you are operating the computer. However, as soon as you switch it off it will return to the default setting. The next time that you switch it on it will show the original margin and command menu. People react in much the same way. When a piece of communication is going well they will respond positively, and be in control of their behaviour. However, when a piece of communication is going badly they will automatically default to the behaviour they learned as a child. So, they will either get angry and shout – *Aggressive*; give in resentfully – *Passive*; or get sarcastic and sulky – *Manipulative*. The communication will break down with both parties feeling bad about themselves and about each other.

ASSERTIVE BEHAVIOUR

Assertive behaviour will help you to manage your communication so that you feel OK about yourself and the person with whom you are communicating. Assertiveness is not natural. It is a skill that is learned. It is based on making *CHOICES* about how you behave. Assertive behaviour means:

- *Making choices*
- *Behaving in an adult way*
- *Believing that you have rights and SO DO OTHERS*
- *Being flexible*

To be effective in communication you need to stop reacting and start choosing. When at traffic lights you react to the red light by braking and to the green light by accelerating. However, when the traffic light is amber you have to make a choice about what to do.

RED   – *Reaction*
AMBER – *Choice*
GREEN – *Reaction*

Assertiveness is the behavioural equivalent to the amber traffic light. You choose to be assertive. Assertiveness is about you *AND* me *NOT* me not you.

1. Aggressive/Manipulative

I'm   You're
OK   Not OK
WIN   **LOSE**

2. Passive

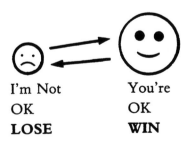

I'm Not   You're
OK   OK
LOSE   **WIN**

3. Assertive

I'm OK   You're OK
WIN   **WIN**

To make communication effective we should be aiming for 'I'm OK, You're OK' depicted in diagram 3.

Assertiveness is about setting a value on yourself and your opinions and on other people and their opinions. Assertive behaviour means behaving in a way that expresses your own feelings, needs and wants while understanding that the other person has their own feelings, needs and wants. Assertiveness means:

- *Respecting yourself*
- *Taking responsibility for yourself*
- *Recognising your own needs and wants independently of others*
- *Making clear 'I' statements*
- *Allowing yourself to make mistakes*
- *Allowing yourself to enjoy your successes*
- *Changing your mind*
- *Asking for 'thinking it over' time*
- *Asking for what you want*
- *Setting clear boundaries*
- *Recognising that you have a responsibility towards others but not **for** others*
- *Respecting other people and recognising that they have the same rights that you do.*

Choosing Behaviour

Recognise that you have the right to choose not to be assertive. However, in making the choice you must take responsibility for the fact that it may result in a situation where neither you nor the other person feels OK and the situation is not resolved. Examine your current behaviours: which most accurately reflect you? Do you:

Hunch up	or	Stand erect
Slouch	or	Face people
Avert your gaze	or	Look people squarely in the face
Balance on one leg	or	Stand firmly and squarely
Shuffle and slip into your workplace	or	Walk confidently
Smile shyly	or	Greet people openly
Tense your features	or	Face people openly in a frank, friendly, and interesting way
Mumble apologetically	or	Speak with authority
Fiddle with your hands	or	Use movements positively
Stand while the other remains seated	or	Have uncrossed legs
Stride about	or	Move closer to the other person
If seated, lean right back with both hands behind your head and legs splayed	or	Lean forward slightly
Lurch forward suddenly	or	Avoid sudden movements
Stare at the other person	or	Look at the other person's face
Have a wry 'I've heard it all before' smile	or	Smile when pleased
Raise your eyebrows in exaggerated amazement or disbelief	or	Nod your head occasionally as the other person is talking
Have your arms crossed	or	Keep arms uncrossed
Have your palms clenched	or	Have open palms

CHOOSE which way you behave, particularly in a conflict or potential conflict situation.

APPROACHING PEOPLE

If you have to approach someone with a complaint, problem or a suggestion follow these basic rules:

- *Identify what you are trying to achieve out of this communication?*
  For example – If you have been given a faulty service by another department you may want to make sure that it doesn't happen again. You will then choose to be assertive because that will help you to achieve your objective. You may decide, however, that you just want to 'have a go' at that department. Bear in mind that although that might relieve your feelings, it is unlikely that the individuals concerned will then take care to make sure that whatever it was that annoyed you doesn't happen again.
- *Ask yourself what their reaction is likely to be? Even though you have approached them assertively they may not always respond in the same way. Be aware of what the alternative reactions might be.*
- *Decide how you might respond to different reactions from the one you want.*
- *Think about what other ways there might be to achieve your objective, particularly if you think that approaching them directly might lead to open confrontation.*
- *Choose the best time and place in which to approach them. First thing on a Monday morning and last thing on a Friday night, particularly if it's a major issue is unlikely to be effective.*
- *Have a 'fallback' position. You will not always get exactly what you want, because people's needs, wants and priorities will not necessarily match your own.*
- *Decide in advance what your limits are and how far you are prepared to*

compromise, if at all. Decide what your action will be if you and the other person cannot come to an agreement.

USING THE RIGHT LANGUAGE

When you are in conflict situations you will have a tendency to do two things:

- *'Blame' and 'accuse' the other person and make them responsible for how you feel and behave.*
- *Write off their entire character rather than dealing with the specific thing which has annoyed or upset you.*

A good example of this is in dealing with partners. Imagine you have decided to prepare a special meal or take your partner out to dinner. You expect them to be home at around 6pm because that's when they normally arrive. However, time passes and they finally turn up at 9.30pm having not rung to let you know that they are going to be late. Your natural reaction is likely to be anger. You may raise your voice and say things like: *'Where the hell have you been? Why didn't you ring, you're always so inconsiderate, you never think about me. You don't care about the fact that I might be worried. You've made me really angry/hurt/upset'*. What you are doing here is attacking the other person's entire character. The fact is, they're not always inconsiderate, they *sometimes* are, they *do* care and think about you, but sometimes they forget. By writing off their entire character you create a situation where they stop listening to you or don't believe they might have been at fault because what you are yelling at them basically isn't true. Harping on about *why* something happened and the *fact* that it happened isn't constructive. What you are looking for here is not a resolution to the conflict but 'blood'!

Whenever you are in a situation where you feel angry or upset it's important to *own* those feelings. They are *your* feelings and only *you* have control over how you deal with them. The best way to deal with conflict is to use the following language:

'*When you* . . .' (do, say, behave in a particular way), '*I feel* . . . (angry, upset, disappointed)'. '*I'd like you to* . . . (whatever action you want in the future)'. By approaching the situation in this way you are:

- *Telling the person specifically what it is they have done*
- *Owning your feelings about what they have done*
- *Focussing on the future which they can affect (ie: saying that* next time you would like them to behave in a different way rather than saying 'You always do this to me!')

In a work situation you may add to the 'I feel' statement something about what happens when they behave in a certain way.

Here are some examples: '*When you come home late from work and don't telephone to let me know* **I feel** *very angry and hurt. I'd like it if next time you would telephone*'.

'*When you come into work late,* **I have** *to take your telephone calls and* **I feel** *angry because that means I can't get on with my own work.* **I'd like** *you to come to work on time.*'

Always use the word that most accurately reflects the way that you really feel. Don't say '*I was a little bit annoyed*' if what you really mean is '*I was livid*'. Don't say '*It doesn't matter*' if it does. Don't say '*perhaps*' or '*maybe*' or '*I'll try*' if what you really mean is '*No*'.

Being assertive doesn't mean just being 'nice'. It means saying honestly and openly how you feel and what you want.

If you feel very angry about something you need to ensure that your words, body language and tone of voice accurately reflect how you are feeling. That doesn't necessarily mean shouting, ranting and raging.

What it actually means is saying '*I feel very angry about this*' and putting emphasis on the word 'angry'.

BODY LANGUAGE

Fifty-five per cent of a message received and understood comes via our body language. The way we stand, sit, gesture, move around gives people information about how we are feeling.

Ensure that you are using the appropriate body language in your communication. For example, if you are upset, smiling deprecatingly will not emphasise your message. Telling someone that you are very pleased with them without an accompanying smile will not have the

same impact. People read body language all the time, subconsciously translating the messages you are sending. How many times have you heard a shop assistant say *'Have a nice day'* and known perfectly well that the last thing that person really wanted was for you to have a nice day. Or heard the expression *'It's not what you said, it's the way that you said it'*.

Ensure that the 'way that you say something' matches the thing that is being said.

IN SUMMARY

Listed below are a number of examples of ways to resolve situations and achieve a win/win outcome.

Information Gathering

- *Explain why you require the information.*
- *Avoid over-justification.*
- *Ask open questions.*
- *Do not interrupt.*
- *Give appropriate non-verbal responses.*
- *Do not respond verbally to every statement the other person makes.*

Information Giving

- *State objectives.*
- *Be direct and to the point.*
- *Avoid over-justification.*
- *Summarise and point the way ahead.*

Disagreeing

- *Clearly identify areas of agreement and disagreement.*
- *Support your ideas with objective evidence if possible.*
- *Avoid personalising your disagreement.*
- *Disagree with what is said, not with the person that is saying it.*
- *Be prepared to change your opinion.*
- *Negotiate a positive solution.*

Example – Someone approaches you saying '*I think that we need another computer in this department*'.

Ineffective Response

'*No we don't. We're never using them enough as it is. You just never manage your time properly. You're totally wrong and I'm not prepared to discuss it.*'

Effective Response

'*You believe we need another computer. I believe we need to manage the way it is used more effectively. Perhaps we could look at some solutions together.*'

Making Requests

- *Be direct and to the point.*
- *Explain why you are making the request. Avoid over-justification, or profuse apologies.*
- *Keep it short and simple.*
- *Avoid manipulation. Let the request stand on its own merits.*
- *Avoid personalising your request.*
- *Be prepared for the other person's refusal.*

Example – You want to borrow someone else's computer.

Ineffective Approach

'I hope you don't mind me asking you this, I know you're terribly busy and I feel terrible asking but I really am up to my eyes and I'm beginning to feel I can't cope. I really need to use your computer tomorrow. Please don't say no, I know you always are really helpful.'

Effective Approach

'Please may I use your computer tomorrow? I miscalculated a deadline and I must get these figures out to departments by the end of the week.'

Refusing Requests

- *Briefly and clearly state what you are willing and unwilling to do.*
- *Avoid making profuse apologies.*
- *Offer an explanation but avoid over-justification.*
- *Keep it short and simple.*
- *Avoid personalising your refusal.*
- *If pressed, repeat your refusal, slowing down and stressing important words.*

Example – Someone asks you if they can borrow your computer tomorrow.

Ineffective Response

'Oh, um, well, actually, I'm really terribly sorry, I'm a bit busy myself, I really need to use it, I'm really really sorry. The thing is, you're always asking to borrow my computer. Can't you ask someone else for a change . . . ?.'

Effective Response

'I'm sorry, I'd like to be able to help, however, I need to use it all day tomorrow for my report. Perhaps, Fred may be able to lend you his.'

RESPONDING TO CONFRONTATION

- *Acknowledge the strength of their feelings.*
- *Acknowledge their needs.*
- *State your needs.*
- *Review facts and options to resolve the issue.*
- *Summarise and point the way ahead.*

Example – You refuse the request to borrow your computer and the person says 'You are really annoying me. I hate it when you refuse a perfectly reasonable request'.

Ineffective Response

'You're the one who's annoying. You're always asking to borrow things. Maybe you ought to manage your own resources a bit better.'

Effective Response

'I can see you're really annoyed about this and I understand that you need to use a computer. However, I need to use it myself tomorrow. Perhaps Fred will be able to lend you his.'

SUMMARY

- *Aim for a WIN/WIN situation.*
- *Take into account the other person's feelings, wants and needs.*
- *Be honest.*
- *Make sure your tone and body language match the words that you use.*
- *Don't 'react' to situations. Make a conscious choice about your behaviour.*

# 7 WORKING WITH OTHERS

Every organisation, large and small, forms itself into a basic structure. Even organisations that are very flexible and cross-functional form themselves into basic working areas where people with similar objectives are based. These normally take the form of departments.

Each department or function will take on an identity within the organisation. People working within the organisation will tend to associate individuals within that department with the identity that it has acquired. Even new people or people who transfer across departments will often find themselves suddenly being treated slightly differently by colleagues. This is because they have now been associated with a department with a different identity.

If you work in a particular department, and have always done so people will assume that you know nothing about anything else other than the work which you undertake. If you work in an Accounts Department people tend to assume that the only thing you know anything about is calculators and that sales or production are completely alien to you. No department is completely isolated. Every department, in order to function effectively itself, has to have some knowledge of how the rest of the organisation operates.

All departments are made up of people and people often have more knowledge than they give themselves credit for – or are given credit for by others.

Organisations are *NOT* about departments. They are about

PEOPLE. How often have you heard someone say: '*The Accounts Department says No*'. The Accounts Department is not a separate entity. It is a group of *people*. It is not the department that has said '*No*', it is an individual within that department who has said no. That means that the decision can be tackled, the person approached, argued with, remonstrated with, persuaded.

When working with other people do not assume that *they* are a 'department'. Treat people as people, regardless of where they work.

GETTING TO KNOW PEOPLE

It is difficult to build up an effective and co-operative relationship with someone that you have never met. Once people have met you they are more likely to give you an identity of your own. People help out their friends. There is nothing wrong with that. To work effectively with people in departments other than your own, build up a friendly relationship with them.

- *Acknowledge their expertise in their own area.*
- *Don't tell them how to do their jobs or compare them to other people/ departments.*
- *Don't give them the same identity as the rest of their department. When they agree to a request you have made don't say 'The Accounts department is so friendly and helpful'. Focus on the individual. Say 'Tim in Accounts is so helpful'.*
- *Get to know them. Visit them in their own departments. Invite them to come and visit you. Instead of sending something in the internal post, take it yourself.*
- *Whenever you visit another department make an effort to speak to at least one or two people. Get into the habit of calling out a cheery 'good morning' to people as you enter the room and a 'see you soon' as you leave.*

- *Smile and thank people if they do something for you, even if it's as simple as telling you where the person you have come to see is located.*

- *If you see someone from another department visiting your own department make the effort to say good morning. It has often amazed me how you can walk into a department, obviously look lost and people ignore you. It doesn't give a very favourable view of the people. You then have a department identity which is one of being unfriendly and unhelpful.*

- *Try and find out exactly what the other departments do during their working day. Ask questions, show interest. In particular ask them what problems they encounter and what you can do in your own department to help reduce their problems.*

- *Stick to the deadlines they have set you. If you have a problem meeting them then let them know IN ADVANCE of the deadline. Don't phone them the day of the deadline and expect them to be sympathetic when you tell them you can't do it. Be realistic – you wouldn't be sympathetic if they didn't let you know!*

- *Don't be afraid to ask for help if you have a problem. People like to be asked to explain things or give advice and assistance.*

DEALING WITH PEOPLE OF DIFFERENT STATUS

I remember an old boss of mine who used to regularly 'walk the job', ie, wander around the building chatting to people, finding out how they were getting on and how business was. This was precisely what he had been told to do when he had been on his management training course. The only problem was that the only people he ever spoke to were the senior people. No-one was impressed, not even those senior people he did talk to because he never made the effort to speak to others in the department. It is *crucial* that you talk to everyone regardless of how important they seem to be. They are people and they talk *about* you if you don't give them the opportunity to talk *to* you. Don't be an organisational snob. **Everyone** is important.

SOCIALISING

Socialising is one of the most effective ways of getting to know people.

Organise a gang of people to go to the pub at Friday lunchtime. You don't have to drink alcohol. The important thing is for people to be sat in a comfortable, friendly atmosphere which encourages informal chatting. You are trying to build up relationships. If you are a manager you are helping your team to build up relationships with people in other parts of the organisation. Organise competitions, like a darts match or rounders or something similar, where departments compete against each other. This not only helps people to get to know each other but encourages healthy competition and team spirit. If you're not the manager there's no reason why you couldn't organise it yourself. If you need to you can always suggest it to your manager to get their support.

INTERNAL CUSTOMER CARE

Good customer care has become important to organisations. In the current world of work there is more competition. What customers are looking for is not just a good product but a good service associated with the product.

Where organisations and people often fall down is in *IN-TERNAL CUSTOMER CARE*. This is treating the people that we work with as customers. Treating them with the same politeness, care and effort that you would accord someone who was actually buying your product or service.

No department can operate independently of another. If you treat people in other departments as you would external customers they are likely to respond in the same way. Your jobs will be made easier and you will be more effective. More importantly, however, you will be *seen* to be more effective and as someone who is helpful, co-operative and gets things done. In practice when dealing with people within the organisation there are some basic rules to follow:

- *Treat every internal person as someone important.*
- *Make time to deal with their problems or queries.*
- *Be honest without being unhelpful and impolite. If you can't help them, say so, give them the reasons why and then always suggest alternatives.*
- *Try to say 'yes' to people.*

- *Get into the habit of negotiating in order to meet your internal customer's demands. If they need something, renegotiate the deadline if it's difficult to meet. Ask for and offer help or suggest alternatives.*
- *Answer internal telephone calls in exactly the same way as you would external calls. Give your FULL name and offer your help.*
- *If you have agreed to do something by a certain deadline then do it – and by that deadline.*
- *When people visit your department greet them as you would an external visitor. Offer them coffee or refreshments.*
- *Try to sort out their problems. Don't immediately say 'It's nothing to do with me' or 'I'm sorry I can't help you.' You can ALWAYS help, even if that help simply means taking a message and passing it on to the person who can sort out the problem. NEVER pass the buck. The most effective and impressive thing you can do is offer to get the problem sorted out by the relevant person and make sure it is. People will remember how helpful you were and will accord you the same help in the future.*
- *Remember that every department is working with its own problems, deadlines, pressures and priorities. They may not always match yours. Try to find out what they are and take them into account when you are dealing with that department.*

YOUR OWN DEPARTMENT

Help people to get to know your department and how it operates by doing the following:

- *When internal people visit who have never been to your department before, introduce them briefly to everyone and give a brief explanation of what each person does.*

  For example, 'May I introduce you to Tim. Tim is the Supervisor of the dataprocessing team and ensures that all data is on the computer within 24 hours. This is Kathy, Margaret, Robert and Phil. They are the dataprocessing team. Kathy deals with X, Margaret with Y, Robert with Z and Phil is on Special Projects'.

This helps people to put jobs and names to faces – it makes the team feel important and impresses the visitor. Better still – get your team to introduce themselves.

- *Draw up a handout briefly explaining the work of your department giving simple details of who to speak to regarding which matter/issue. List every member of staff by their full names with their extension number and a brief description of their jobs and key responsibilities.*

If money permits include a photograph and circulate the handout. Send it out with a memo saying why you are sending it.

EXAMPLE

MEMORANDUM

TO: ALL HEADS OF DEPARTMENT
FROM: FRED
DATE: 17 NOVEMBER 1993

COMPUTER DEPARTMENT
I thought you might find it useful and help you to sort out problems and queries more quickly and effectively if you had a handout on the work of my department and the people who work within it. etc. . . .

INTER-DEPARTMENTAL COMPETITION

Every organisation suffers from inter-departmental competition. Usually it is unhealthy and unproductive. A colleague of mine,

Alan Martin, gave me the following illustration which you could share with your colleagues.

Imagine two football teams playing a match, Team X and Team Y. Within each team each player has a particular responsibility. The goalkeeper's function is to protect and defend the goal. The centre forward's job is to score goals and so on.

During the match each team member performs their own function. Sometimes, by chance, the goalkeeper sees an opportunity to score a goal and seizes it. You don't then find the rest of the X team protesting to the referee *'That's not his/her job, he/she shouldn't be scoring goals, tell him/her not to do it ever again, in fact it should be disallowed.'*

On the contrary! The team is much more likely to make a big fuss of the goalkeeper for being clever enough to spot the opportunity and take advantage of it. If while the goalkeeper is too far away from the goal mouth the centre forward saves a goal from being scored by the opposition, the rest of the team doesn't say *'That's not his/her job, he/she shouldn't have done that, he/she shouldn't have saved that goal – you should give it to Y team'*. If a member of the team is in possession of the ball and surrounded by the opposition you don't see the rest of his/her team hanging back saying *'it's his/her problem, nothing to do with me, not my job, he/she got him/herself into it, he/she should get him/herself out of it'*.

A football team works as a team – each member having their own responsibilities, but there to help out and support each other against the opposition. **The same should be true for organisations**. Yet how often do you hear people in organisations bitching about other departments or complaining about the fact the other department is encroaching on their territory. Or grumbling because they have to do something that they consider to be the work of the other department. THIS IS RIDICULOUS!

At the end of the day, it's one team, one organisation and every department within that organisation needs to be successful for the whole

organisation to be successful. And that means everybody needs to help
and support everyone else.

SUMMARY

- *Always offer to help other departments whenever you can.*
- *Don't bad-mouth other departments or people within those departments.*
- *Face the fact that there is not a huge amount that you can do about the approach and behaviour of other people in other departments, but you can do something about your behaviour and that of the rest of your team.*

8 MAKING CHANGE HAPPEN

Sometimes you will be put in a position at work where you have to make change happen, either because you have been asked to or because it's your own idea and you want to implement it.

WHAT CAUSES CHANGE?

Change is constant and normal. In today's world only organisations that are open to and encourage change are the ones that survive. Just as animals constantly adapt to their environments in order to survive, so too do organisations need to adapt to the environment around them in order to survive successfully. Change is caused by:

- **New Technology** – *needing different ways of working*
- **Competition** – *other organisations selling products/services similar to or superior to our own. A smaller marketplace means more competition. Small businesses being set up which offer a cheaper and more personal service to the customer.*
- **Market Demands** – *Customers wanting higher quality goods at a lower price. A more sophisticated market – made more demanding by the amount of choice available.*
- **Education** – *a higher educated, more demanding staff as well as customers. This means higher expectations.*
- **Aspirations** – *With the advent of new laws, new technology, increased*

marketing and advertising, people are more aware of what's on offer, both career-wise and consumer-wise. Therefore their aspirations are higher.

WHY DO PEOPLE RESIST CHANGE?

People like to feel secure. They want certain things to be fixed. Basic motivation theory says that people need food, shelter and warmth. If those basic needs are met then they are more receptive to other things. It's the same at work. People need to know that they have somewhere to sit. A desk that belongs to them. A guarantee that they will be paid. An assurance that they aren't likely to lose their jobs. A belief that they are valued in the job that they do.

People will resist change if they feel threatened by it. Most people do feel threatened by change. Change means that what was familiar will become unfamiliar. People fear that they may not do as well in jobs that have changed. The only people who don't feel threatened by change are the people whose idea it was in the first place.

OVERCOMING RESISTANCE

To overcome people's resistance to change you need to make them feel that they own the change by involving them in the implementation of it. Involve by consulting. Consultation is NOT explaining what the change is and asking people to agree. *REAL* consultation means explaining the objective you want to achieve and *asking* people for their suggestions and ideas as to how to get there. Say something like: 'I want to change X to Y for the following reasons. I have some ideas as to how to achieve this and they are A, B, C. I'd really appreciate any other suggestions you might have and any comments and ideas as to how I can achieve this.'

If your boss, your colleagues or your team suggest ideas make sure you take them seriously and if you possibly can, implement them. When presenting change:

- *Acknowledge people's fears and worries. Don't dismiss them.*
- *Acknowledge weaknesses in your own arguments.*
- *Instead of defending your position to criticism, ask people if they can come up with alternative suggestions. If you ask people for alternatives and they can't come up with any practical ones they are more likely to follow your suggestions.*
- *Give credit to people who had some input into your idea.*
- *When presenting the idea give some flesh to the bones. People will pull apart and change some things but your basic skeleton will remain unchanged. If you don't do this you may find the core of your plan has been changed.*
- *Have alternative suggestions available. If people are clearly against one particular aspect of your idea/plan you have something to fall back on.*

GENERATING IDEAS

There are some simple techniques for generating new ideas. Think laterally. Let go of any preconceived notions or ideas that you have. They will only hamper you in arriving at a solution or generating ideas. For example, join up all nine of these dots with four straight lines. Most of you will be unable to do it.

The solution is on page 119.

•　　　•　　　•

•　　　•　　　•

•　　　•　　　•

The reason you couldn't do it is because the nine dots gave the appearance of a box. You assumed that you could only draw the lines within the box. Yet in the instructions I gave, nowhere did I say that you had to stay within the box shape. You may sometimes take a similar approach at work. You assume constraints exist without ever really checking them out.

Common phrases are '*My boss would never allow it*'. '*It would probably cost too much*'. '*I'd never get it through*'. '*We can't ask people to change what they're already doing*'. '*We have to have such and such as a product*'. What you are actually doing is preventing yourself from being successful before you even begin. Try to solve the following puzzle by thinking laterally.

- *You are playing golf and with one of your shots you hit the ball into a paper bag. How can you get the ball out of the bag without touching either the ball or the bag?*

Answer on page 119.

BRAINSTORMING

Brainstorming is a way of harnessing the creativity and ideas of people. Brainstorming is a word that gets misused. People use it to describe meetings where ideas are batted around. True brainstorming has a simple and clear technique which needs to be followed in order to make it most effective. If the rules aren't followed brainstorming doesn't work properly.

- *Use a flipchart.*
- *At the top of the flipchart write down what it is you are trying to achieve. For example,* **increase income by £5000 per month**

- *Set a time limit, eg, 20 minutes.*
- *Go round each person in turn asking them for their ideas.*
- *Do not allow people just to shout out ideas. Go round systematically. If someone can't think of anything then they say 'Pass' and you move on to the next person.*
- *Write down EXACTLY what each person says – don't modify it.*
- *DO NOT ask any questions at this stage.*
- *DO NOT get into discussions about any one idea.*
- *At the end of the 20 minutes stop the brainstorming session. Then go through each point deciding how likely or unlikely it is to help achieve your original objective.*
- *When you are left with a few ideas you are now in a position to decide exactly how you want to proceed or to research and investigate the ideas before deciding which one to go along with.*

SUMMARY

- *Regularly talk to the people involved in the change to get their feedback.*
- *If any problems are identified don't dismiss them. Tackle them and sort them out.*
- *Keep people regularly informed and updated: the boss, your team, your colleagues, anyone who is affected by the change.*
- *Keep an open mind. If the change clearly isn't working then be prepared to change your mind or admit that you made an error of judgment.*
- *Keep a note of successes as well as failures. Share them with people.*
- *Have a clear written down plan with deadlines broken down into smaller deadlines. When planning make sure that you work **backwards** from the deadline leaving time for things to go wrong.*
- *Make sure that individuals are clear exactly who is responsible for what. Who will be monitoring their progress and how often. Who they should go to if they have a problem.*

 # MOVING UP THE ORGANISATION

Not everyone wants to be promoted or move 'up' the organisation. Some of you reading this book may feel perfectly happy and contented with the level that you are at – and that's absolutely fine. Don't let anyone make you feel that you are under-achieving if you are happy to remain where you are doing what you are doing.

The reality is that the further up an organisation you go the more likely it is that your working life is going to start encroaching on your home and personal life. Only *you* can make the decision as to how you wish to balance your life.

If you are keen to progress 'upwards' there are 3 things you need to do:

- *Develop yourself – expand your knowledge and skills*
- *Get to know the right people.*
- *Demonstrate your ability.*

DEVELOP YOURSELF

The higher up the management ladder that you move the more you will be required to have a breadth of skills, understanding and knowledge. Senior managers need to have a good commercial awareness, financial ability, people management skills, communication skills and an ability to think strategically. To be able to look well ahead and let go of the day to day running of the organisation. They also need to have a good understanding of how all the departments/functions that make up the whole organisation work and how they all contribute to the corporate picture. To prepare yourself for a more senior position:

- *Attend relevant training courses. Put into* action *what you have learned.*
- *Read the annual report of your organisation.*
- *Get involved in internal projects.*
- *Get a professional qualification.*
- *Take a secondment for a few weeks or months to another department or organisation.*
- **Read!** *Magazines, trade journals, books relevant to the running of your organisation.*
- *Watch the news, read quality newspapers.* Don't *be seen reading the tabloid press. Make sure you have a knowledge of current affairs.*
- *Don't wait for someone to 'develop' you. Decide what you want to do and do it.*
- *Make sure you know how your organisation is doing financially. Read the accounts.*
- *Keep an eye on what your competitors are doing.*
- *Get involved in training other people.*
- *Offer to take on board some of your boss's responsibilities.*
- *Delegate tasks to your team and other colleagues.*
- *Be competent and confident at handling and using computers.*
- *Attend social gatherings and functions.*
- *Watch TV documentaries.*
- *Get involved in your local community. Become a school governor or a treasurer of a local society.*
- *Develop your experience and understanding of other departments by finding out what they do.*
- *Apply for jobs to demonstrate your keenness to get on. Get some practice at being interviewed.*

GET TO KNOW THE RIGHT PEOPLE

Imagine this situation. You are a senior manager who is recruiting for a position. You have a choice between two candidates, both internal. One of them you know fairly well, you have come across them at meetings or social gatherings. You have seen copies of reports they have done, have had suggestions and ideas put to you by them. The second is one that you don't know at all. Their references and work history look impressive. Which one are you likely to select?

Most people will select the person that they know. If you know the way someone approaches their job and have found them to be effective and helpful you will recruit that person over one you don't personally know.

Once, when I was recruiting for a secretary I had a choice between two candidates both of whom I knew fairly well. One candidate was extremely impressive in the interview stage. However, I had seen this person doing their current job and I knew that the words didn't necessarily match the actions. The other candidate was clearly very nervous and didn't come across as well in the interview, but I had also seen this person in action and had always been impressed. So the second candidate got the job, because I had seen for myself in the way they had handled their previous job, how they were likely to tackle the new one.

At work people are promoted because they have been seen to prove their ability by others at higher levels who have the power to promote. Getting to know the right people means doing the following:

- *Speak to **everyone** in the organisation as if they are all equal.*
- *Attend social functions/gatherings.*
- *Visit other departments – get to know the people.*
- *Involve yourself in projects.*

- *Make a point of greeting people (again **everyone**) as you pass them in the corridor, on the stairs or in the lift.*
- *Thank people if they have helped you, both verbally and by memo. Send a copy of a thank you memo to the person's boss. Think how good you would feel if someone did that for you.*
- *Turn up at meetings on time and well prepared.*
- *If you are asked your views be honest. Don't tell people what you think they want to hear. They'll soon find out that you weren't telling them the truth.*
- *Put forward objections and/or complaints constructively.*
- *Have suggested solutions or options that could be pursued.*
- *Be a 'volunteer'. Offer to help out, even if it's not your own department that needs the help. This will help you to expand your knowledge of the organisation and impress others.*

DEMONSTRATE YOUR ABILITY

Value your own achievements and blow your own trumpet. Don't wait for other people to do it for you.

It's a question of balance. Bosses don't necessarily want to receive copies of every 'happy' letter you ever receive. However, they will want to hear about your achievements and that of your team and colleagues.

- *Make sure that you draw the boss's attention to the achievements of others, as well as your own.*
- *Carry out the actions listed in all the chapters in this book.*
- *Don't be afraid to ask questions. Make appointments to see the boss to discuss particular issues.*
- *Find yourself a mentor. Someone who you can talk over problems and issues with and who will give you honest feedback.*
- *Don't get involved in politics. Don't take sides. Formulate your own view and be honest about it when asked. Maintain your personal integrity. Don't get involved in back-biting and pettinesses.*

- *Look at what senior managers do and how they behave. Pick up the things that you think are good and emulate them.*

There's a story about a person who was just about to be appointed a general. They were nervous about this and expressed their fear to their partner about their being taken seriously and treated like a general. The partners response was: '*Act like a general, dress like a general, speak like a general, look like a general – and you'll be a general*'.

This is common sense advice. Behave in the way in which you would like others to see you.

- *Say 'No' to things that you really feel are inappropriate for you to do.*
- *Be prepared (but only if it's necessary) to come in early and or work late on occasion if that's what's needed to get the job done.*

Above all don't whinge about having to work late. If you don't want to do it then DON'T.

HOW TO BE SUCCESSFUL AT INTERVIEWS

If you are presented with an opportunity for promotion you will be judged as much on how well you conduct yourself at the interview as on past performance. The key to a successful interview is **preparation**.

Preparation

- *Research thoroughly everything you can about the job and the department.*
- *Speak to the person who currently holds the job. Find out exactly what it entails and what problems they have.*
- *In a notebook make lots of notes on the information you have found out.*
- *Think of as many creative ideas as you can and jot them in your notebook to put forward at the interview.*

- *In the notebook write down a minimum of 10 questions for you to ask the interviewer.*
- *Try and find out what questions you are likely to be asked. If no one can tell you, then use your common sense. Imagine yourself in the shoes of the interviewer and anticipate the questions that you might be asked and prepare your answers.*
- *Type up a brief description of your major achievements, your strengths and any ideas you might have to give to the interviewer. This is in addition to whatever information they may already have eg, your CV, personnel file.*
- *Dress in the style which fits the job you are applying for rather than the job you are currently in.*

During the Interview

- *Take your notebook in with you and make notes during the interview.*
- *Use your notebook as reference. If you are asked a question and you need time to answer it then refer to your notes.*
- *If the interviewer answers a question that you had written down, cross it off your list. Do it obviously so that the interviewer can see that you have thoroughly prepared.*
- *Take your time answering questions.*
- *Don't feel you have to have an answer for every question. Waffling is nearly always obvious. If you don't know the answer then say so.*
- *At the end of the interview run through your notes and make sure that you have said everything you wanted to.*

After the Interview

- *Send a letter to the interviewer thanking them for the interview. Even if you don't get the job at the very least you have gained valuable interview experience and raised your profile.*

SUMMARY

- *Broaden your general knowledge.*
- *Get to know people in other departments.*
- *Find yourself a mentor and a role model.*
- *Prepare thoroughly for interviews.*

10 LOOKING THE PART

In being effective at work, ultimately you will be judged by your results, that is, producing the work you are expected to produce, on time and to the highest quality. Having said that, it is important not to minimise the effect that your appearance, language and approach has on your ability to be effective. Some people seem to be successful without appearing to make any particular effort. It all comes naturally to them. Then there are others, who despite help, support and encouragement never seem to get anywhere. This book has talked a lot about how others see you. But the most important perception of all is the perception that you have of yourself. If you see yourself as a winner you will be a winner. If you see yourself as a loser, then you will probably be a loser.

As people go through their lives, both working and personal, they meet problems and disappointments. Each time a setback is encountered it activates a tape recorder in the brain which is called the 'Loser' tape. This tape activates every time you are in a vulnerable position. The tape makes you doubt your ability, limit your initiative and destroy your self confidence. The 'Loser' tape switches on automatically. 'Winner' tapes on the other hand are the ones you consciously switch on to overcome your 'Loser' tape. 'Winner' tapes reinforce your self confidence, your belief in your ability and your willingness to keep trying until you succeed.

HOW TO IDENTIFY YOUR WINNER/LOSER TAPES

A winner says:	A loser says:
Life is good to me	Nothing ever goes my way
Yes I will/No I won't	Yes . . . perhaps . . . maybe
I'll find time to do it	How do you expect me to find time to do it
Let's sort this out	I can't do anything
I haven't explained myself clearly	You didn't listen/you don't understand
We have different views	I'm not changing my mind
I'm OK, but there is still room for improvement	I'm not as bad as the others
Tell me . . .	How many times do I have to tell you?
There must be a better way	We've always done it this way
Let's be more flexible	The memo said . . .
Let's work on a presentation to the management	Management will never agree to that
You learn something new every day	What about all my years of experience.
Let's make it work this time	I told you it wouldn't work
That sounds exciting	Why keep changing things?
What do you think/feel/want?	Nobody ever listens to me
Let me see if I can sort it out	It's not my job/problem

WINNER AND LOSER BEHAVIOURS

Winners:	Losers:
Work harder and have more time	Are always too busy
Go straight to the heart of a problem	Go round the problem and never solve it
Make commitments	Promise too readily
Know when to fight hard and when to give way	Give way on important issues or hold on to things that aren't worth fighting for
Feel strong enough to be friendly	Are rarely friendly
Listen	Wait for their turn to talk
Respect others' strengths	Focus on others weaknesses
Learn from others	Are resistant to others
Explain	Make excuses
Feel responsible for more than just their own work	Say 'That's not my job'
Set their own pace	Have only two speeds, flat out or dead slow
Use time to improve	Use time to avoid trouble
Aren't afraid of making and admitting mistakes	Are afraid of making mistakes and of what others will say
Focus on possibilities and solutions	Focus on problems and unresolvable issues.

SUMMARY

- *Whenever you are in a situation where you feel vulnerable and there is a danger that your 'Loser' tape will start playing consciously switch on your 'Winner' tape.*
- *Remind yourself of the programming cycle mentioned in Chapter 1. You can break the cycle by behaving differently.*
- *Don't be a cynic, no matter how tempting it is. Cynics don't change things.*

ANSWERS TO PUZZLES

Page 105

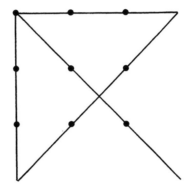

Page 106

You are playing golf and with one of your shots you hit the ball into a paper bag. How can you get the ball out of the bag without touching either the ball or the bag?

ANSWER: Set fire to the bag.   This takes the bag away from the ball rather than trying to take the ball out of the bag.

BIBLIOGRAPHY

I'm OK, You're OK
Harris, Thomas A., M.D. (Pan, rev 1973)

Leaders: The Learning Curve of Achievement
Forrest, A. and Tolfree, P. (The Industrial Society, 1992)

Letters At Work
Barker, A. (The Industrial Society, 1993)

The Right Report
Barker, A. (The Industrial Society, 1993)

Assertiveness: A Working Guide
O'Brien, P. (Nicholas Brealey Publishing, 1991)